Gisbert Greshake

THE MEANING OF CHRISTIAN PRIESTHOOD

The Meaning of Christian Priesthood

———◦◦◦◦◦◦———

GISBERT GRESHAKE

Translated by Fr Peadar MacSeumais, SJ

WITH A FOREWORD BY
Robert F. Morneau
AUXILIARY BISHOP OF GREEN BAY

CHRISTIAN CLASSICS
Westminster, Maryland
1989

First published in U.S.A., 1989

This translation of *Priestersein* (Herder:
Freiburg . Basle . Vienna, 1982) was
made by Fr Peadar MacSeumais, SJ.
and is published by
Four Courts Press Ltd, Kill Lane, Blackrock, Co. Dublin.

Library of Congress Catalog Card Number: 89-061357

ISBN: 0-87061-168-2
Printed in U.S.A.

Contents

Foreword

A subcommittee of the National Conference of Catholic Bishops' Committee on Priestly Life and Ministry recently issued a document entitled "Reflections on the Morale of Priests." This descriptive essay articulates a number of present factors that affect the morale of priests: false expectations, shortage of personnel, overwork, lack of understanding. The document is not meant to be a theological treatise on priesthood but a brief statement of what many priests are actually experiencing as they valiantly attempt to minister in a complex and pluralistic world.

Documents on morale are needed but also theological reflection on the nature and mission of priesthood. Gisbert Greshake has contributed to the theological enterprise with this studied text, *The Meaning of Christian Priesthood*. Professor Greshake, an experienced teacher and pastoral minister, focuses in on two foundational issues: the trinitarian basis for ordained ministry and the spiritual life of the priest. These two facets of priesthood are intrinsically woven together.

The author extracts many assertions from Scripture, tradition, Church documents and the writings of contemporary theologians. A basic thesis for Professor Greshake is that the priests -- the office-bearer -- must be viewed christologically as acting in the place of Christ and pneumatologically as acting in the name of the Church. Ordination positions the priests in a twofold relationship. It is in the name of Christ that the priest transmits to the people of God the mysteries of salvation. The second relationship is to the Church, "whose faith he (the priest) recapitulates, over whose celebrations he presides and whose unity he manifests."

This double relationship is grounded in the priest's spiritual life. Emphasizing the centrality of imitating Christ through the practice of the evangelical counsels and through service, the author states further that holiness is deepened through a commitment to prayer, study, spiritual reading, pastoral ministry and supportive fraternity.

The formal deliberation of the Second Vatican Council ended twenty-five years ago. Yet as recently as December, 1988, Pope John Paul II issued a major apostolic exhortation ("Christifideles Laici") on the nature and mission of the laity in Church and in the world. In that document the Pope addresses again the relationship of the laity and the mystery of the priesthood, common and ministerial. We continue as a Church to reflect upon the depth of this great gift and grace: priesthood in the Church.

The Meaning of Christian Priesthood presents a perspective of priesthood based on a trinitarian analysis and a specific ecclesiology. Its contribution to the theological conversation enriches our understanding and invites each of us to examine more consciously our life in Christ. Despite the limits of any theological reflection, we are provided an opportunity of reviewing the large questions which shape our ministry in the Church today.

+ Robert F. Morneau
Auxiliary Bishop of
Green Bay, Wisconsin
March 1, 1989

Introduction

This book originated in lectures given at meetings of priests of the archdiocese of Vienna, and at seminars of the Austrian Regents Conference. The response to these lectures, and discussions (especially with theology students), confirm that there is a need in the Church today for a deeper examination of priesthood. Against the background of contemporary debate and a welter of contradictory theological assertions about priesthood, my aim in these pages is to outline an image of the priest which corresponds to Holy Scripture and church tradition and is at the same time appropriate to the needs of contemporary society and the present position of theological research on the subject. I hope that one result of this study will be to provide guidelines for priestly life; my research into the meaning of priesthood is not meant to be an academic exercise: it refers to the lifestyle of the priest himself — the form his service takes, and the way he actually practises his faith: in a word, his spiritual life. Looked at from the other direction, priestly spirituality must be in keeping with the nature of (priestly) ministry or office in the Church, as this ministry is depicted for us in Scripture and Tradition. No one enters on the way to becoming a priest from a position of neutrality; no one designs this vocation for himself; every priest is called to an already existing form of life and service. Thus, just as the ministry of a priest is directed towards an appropriate form of spiritual life, so also his life and spirituality must correspond to the pre-existing nature of that ministry. In this discussion of the nature of priesthood, therefore, I want to consider both theory and practice together; and although there is more emphasis on theological theory in the first part of the book, and on spiritual practice in the second part, I have tried throughout to integrate the two together as much as possible.

The book also aims to reconcile what at first seem to be opposing theological interpretations of priestly office — what I might describe as 'artificial alternatives'. P. Hünernamm has recently described one of the most striking pairs of alternatives (which he also seeks to reconcile) in the following way: 'In the documents of the Second Vatican Council, and still more clearly in theological discussions today, there are to be found two typical concepts of priestly office. The first regards priesthood as a continuation of the mission of Jesus Christ: the priest represents Jesus Christ for the community. The second concept looks on the priesthood as a development of the mystery of the Church; it is the way in which the Church articulates itself and makes itself manifest — the means by which the faith of the Church is transmitted. To say that the priest represents Christ, and that the priest represents the Church, may perhaps be an oversimplification, but it makes clear the distinction between these two concepts'.

These alternatives — Am I a priest of the Church or a priest of Jesus Christ? — have important consequences for a priest's concept of himself, especially when they are so radicalised that he asks, 'Does my ministry consist in the delegation to me by the community/Church of certain tasks and functions; or does it mean that the Lord has by my ordination called me and empowered me to be a spiritual transmitter of his saving work to other Christians?'

These two concepts of priesthood are today being presented as irreconcilable opposites — not only in theological controversy but in terms of the day-to-day life of the priest. In view of this fundamental tension, which gives rise to many problems, I should like to propose my own theological solution, which I might describe as a 'trinitarian concept of priesthood'. Like many other propositions, assertions and arguments in this book, my solution is dependent on the work and suggestions (both positive and negative) of many other theologians; these I have quoted or at least named.* This is an example, one of many in the history of theology, of what Bernard of Chartres refers to when he says, 'We are like

---

*Professor Greshake has agreed to the translator's suggestion that in the English edition the notes be shortened in view of the fact that many of the sources quoted are not easily accessible to English-speaking readers. In most cases this shortening takes the form of merely giving (in parentheses in the text) the name of the author quoted. Full details can be found in the original German edition.

dwarfs standing on the shoulders of giants: that is why we can sometimes see further and more widely than they do'.

A final remark about the precise subject-matter of the book: it is *priesthood as such*. Differences between the various steps in the reception of Holy Orders — (deacon), priest and bishop — are dealt with only marginally.

For help in producing this book I wish to thank in particular Jacob Kremer, who has reviewed the most important exegetical sections and made many suggestions; my assistants Elfi-Maria Lehner and Dr Erwin Rotter, OSB, who have also offered helpful criticism; and Mrs Maria Smeja, who prepared the typescript with her usual devotion and patience. To all these I offer my sincere thanks.

I dedicate this book firstly to all those theology students who are courageously following along the road to the priesthood, often against the resistance of their own families and the pressure of public opinion, and in spite of attempts to unsettle them. I dedicate it secondly to those unknown colleagues who, in the darkness of faith and amid attacks on it, often 'hoping against hope' in the face of failure, still remain loyal to their unglamorous task and way of life, humble as Peter was before he was given his pastoral office: 'Lord, thou knowest all things: thou knowest that I love thee' (Jn 21:17).

G. G.

PART ONE
Towards a theological definition of priesthood

1

Priesthood in crisis

1. 'Everything is tottering' (Ernst Troeltsch).

A crisis can be brought about by talk. One can select elements in a situation which are debatable, distorted and apparently contradictory, and write them up as a crisis — failing to notice that they may only be superficial phenomena, which do not affect the central, let alone the total, reality under discussion. For some years now people have been saying — at least in the West — that the priesthood is in a state of crisis. True, this is more than a crisis brought about by talk — although the media are happy to overlook the fact that there are large numbers of priests who still seek to live their life of service with obvious confidence in their vocation and in the assured help of the Spirit promised at their ordination.

Nevertheless the facts speak a harsh and inescapable message. There is an increasing shortage of priests, due to the reluctance of young men to enter the priestly ministry in its present form; many men have resigned from the priesthood; and there are others who show signs of exhaustion, who are overworked and under excessive psychological stress; in addition there are complaints and protests against episcopal and papal authority and against a form of life and vocation which is felt to be outmoded and unendurable; and finally there is public opinion which, even in so-called good Catholic families, takes the form of an aloof if not a negative attitude to the priestly vocation. What St Paul wrote about his apostolate has relevance for the priest to-day: 'We are made as the refuse of this world, the offscouring of all, even until now' (1 Cor 4:13).

Many causes have been suggested for these signs of crisis in the priesthood. Attention has been drawn to the general movement away from the Church (whatever this may be), and to the lack of interest in religion prevalent in a secularised society which is bent on material progress and is no longer moulded by the Christian ethic: many — and the most important and decisive — insights, values and norms of the Christian faith are not reflected in our society and find no acceptance in it. To be or to become a Christian is widely seen as swimming against the tide. This has a decisive effect on the work of a priest and his concept of himself. Formerly, in a society characterised by Christian faith, he had his predetermined and recognised place of importance as part of an institution. Now, on the contrary, religion is banished more and more into the private sphere of the individual. This means that the position once held by the parish priest among prominent members of society, such as the local mayor, teacher, doctor, solicitor, chemist, is no more. Most people view him as a kind of salesman, promoting something which few seem to want to buy. At least in the advanced industrial society of the West, he no longer has that positive social image which used to give him public status, legitimation and also — extending far beyond the religious and ecclesiastical sphere — the prestige and the security of an institution.

In addition to this, the profile of the priest has become blurred even inside the Church. On account of the new 'opening to the world' officially sanctioned by Vatican II's Constitution *Gaudium et spes*, the liturgical sphere, which for centuries was closely linked to the image of the Catholic priest, has receded into the background, quite contrary to the Council's intention. The 'cosmic liturgy' — the mission of the Church to reshape the world, a mission shared in by each baptised Christian — seems to have become the Church's key role, while in contrast the sacred functions of the priest and his celibate lifestyle, withdrawn from the world, have lost meaning and plausibility.

The modern slogan of 'Democracy everywhere' has taken on an almost sacred quality, as if it were a revelation. The result is that even spiritual authority is being pressurised to justify itself. Moreover, all modern sociological theory, which is particularly penetrated by the idea of equality, is radically opposed to the theological notion of a hierarchy of office and authority. Consequently, many contemporaries [in Germany] find the word *Amt* (office, ministry) extremely embarrassing and altogether unacceptable. Although in its original Celtic form (*ampaht*) it simply means 'service', it has in modern German developed connotations of superiority, dominion and power. As a result quite a number of priests and theologians prefer the world *Dienst* (service), which emphasises the functional aspect of their work — concerning others and for others —, and reject everything which smacks of precedence or elitism. G. Schmidtchen in a research paper on priests in Germany reports that a new and different understanding of spiritual ministry has developed. Although some of the clergy — mainly but not exclusively the older clergy — see their ordination and particular mission from Christ as the justification of their office — a legitimation 'from above' — others feel that they are supported 'from below' through their service to fellow-Christians and by *their* trust and agreement. The result is a division between a 'vertical' and a 'horizontal' concept of priestly office, resulting in a polarisation of the two and a further feeling of insecurity on both sides.

The new pastoral services undertaken by the laity, which include many duties formerly belonging to the clergy, have also produced uncertainty and disagreement about the role of the priest. The priest is forced to ask himself: 'What really is my specific role now?'

All this indicates that today's crisis of the priestly office is basically a crisis of identity. Not a few priests, and very many lay people, have no clear idea of the essential and central nature of priesthood, of the specific mission and task proper to the priest. The priest himself and anyone who is considering becoming a priest have been to a great extent left to work out their own answer to this question. In fact, as far as the understanding of the nature of ecclesiastical office is concerned, theology and the Church have in recent years resembled, and still resemble, a building which is in a state of reconstruction and one can say without too much exaggeration that everyone is concentrating on those parts of the building which interest him most.

The very way of posing the question has noticeably changed. In the *Kirchenlexicon* (1891) the entry under 'layman' is '*see* clergy': in other words, one hundred years ago, 'layman' still needed to be defined, and was in fact defined by reference to 'clergy', which was at that time taken as being self-explanatory. By denying to the layman the specific ordination and power of jurisdiction proper to the cleric, it was possible to define him concisely as 'not a cleric'. Today the contrary is true: 'It is no longer the layman who needs to be defined, but the priest' (Y. Congar), and the priest is defined (or defines himself) by contrasting himself with the layman — the term 'lay' being now apparently self-explanatory. The question now is: What is the difference between a priest and a committed Christian layman (to say nothing of a full-time pastoral assistant)? Is it that the priest has certain special sacred powers which are reserved to him alone, or is he no more than an official of the institution (the Church)? Is it his office of leadership that defines him — and if so, what precisely does this mean? Is it principally his particular personal calling — what indeed is 'calling'? — or is it his special lifestyle (celibacy)?

Given these questions, problems and differences in outlook, which have been debated — inconclusively — in recent years, one can certainly say that as far as the notion of priesthood is concerned 'Everything is tottering'. This dictum of Ernst Troeltsch is rather like Heraclitus' *Panta rhei*: everything is in flux'; and just as Troeltsch has linked the words of Heraclitus with the words of Archimedes, 'Give me a fulcrum and I will move the world', so we also are faced with the question: If everything is tottering, where is the fixed centre of the priest's office which characterises and supports the holder of that office? Where is the central and identifying feature which makes it possible to carry out this ministry, so vital for the Church, even in a situation of spiritual upheaval, and in the absence of a pre-established and fixed role?

2. Post-Vatican II change

To understand the current theological 'reconstruction' I have referred to and the 'existential problems of the priest', (there is in fact a book with that title), we need to recall the profound changes which have occurred in the Church as far as ministry is concerned.

For centuries, the position of the clergy in the Church was unassailed — and the special position of the priest *vis-à-vis* the layman was clearly recognised. Gratian, the father of canon law (*c.* 1160), sums up the medieval position and traces future development in these words: 'There are two kinds of Christian. One is assigned to the service of God, to meditation and prayer, and must keep himself apart from all worldly turmoil. Such are the clerics and the men consecrated to God, i.e. the monks. The other Christians are laity. They are permitted to possess earthly goods, but only for necessary use. . . They are allowed marry, to farm land, to settle complaints by recourse to a judge . . ., to lay offerings on the altar, to pay tithes.In this way they also can be saved, on the condition that they avoid evil while doing good.' In this text priestly ministry (and also the order of monks) is clearly distinguished from the position of the laity and is in fact described as the 'proper' actualisation of Christian life. Furthermore, at least since the high Middle Ages, the priestly ministry was thought of as part of a hierarchical church order or even world order. According to this view, God distributes his *virtus* (the gift and power of life) through a hierarchy: the higher beings, like a fountain, pass on this *virtus* to those below. These higher beings included, in the spiritual sphere, the holders of church office — also arranged in a hierarchy — and in the secular sphere, kings and nobles. A ministry hierarchically organised was seen as indispensable for the reception of the divine gift of salvation and for its transmission to the laity. The superiority and special position of the clergy consisted in this.

The strict distinction which this concept draws between the ministry and the laity was further emphasised by the teaching of the Council of Trent. In interpreting Trent it must of course be remembered that the Council had to defend itself against a levelling (actual or presumed) of the priestly office with the 'universal priesthood' and against replacement of the function and jurisdiction of the priest by the office of preaching. To counter these two challenges, Trent defended the priesthood as it was actually operating in the Church. It was not equipped to put forward a nuanced and balanced teaching about priesthood, and it did not wish to do so. In reply to the argument that there was no such thing as a special priestly office, the Council emphasised the special hierarchical nature of church office, endowed with a specific spiritual jurisdiction. Against the denial of a sacramental character conferred on the priest, it stressed the link between the visible sacrifice (the Mass) and cultic and priestly authority. Thus, Trent continued on the lines already noticeable in the Middle Ages and taught that the priest was principally to be understood from his cultic and sacramental duties and powers, especially from the celebration of the Eucharist.[1] Thus were produced the narrow and onesided canons and the extremely questionable statements of the Pius V Catechism: 'Since the bishops and priests represent ... on earth the person of God himself, their office is obviously of such a kind that no greater can be conceived. Consequently they will rightly be called, not angels merely, but also gods, since they represent for us the numinous power of God' (II, 7, 2). The teaching of Trent later led to the belief that the priest is above all 'the man of the sacraments' and is distinguished from the laity both as 'God's representative' and possessor of cultic authority, and also as a man of special holiness. This basic concept gave its stamp to the spirituality of the priest, his seminary training and his style of life.

Shortly before the Second Vatican Council this image of the priest was once again summarised under Pius XII in the Encyclical *Mediator Dei*: 'Just as Baptism marks all Christians as such and distinguishes them from all others who have not been cleansed in the bath of purification and are not members of Christ, so in a similar way the sacrament of Holy Orders divides the priest from all other Christians who are not endowed with this grace.' For this reason, the priest's life — as the Encyclical *Menti Nostrae* says — should also be more 'free from all sins, hidden with Christ in God' than the life of the lay Christian.

Doctrine on the nature of the Church was developed more and more during the Counter-Reformation into a separate section of theology, in keeping with this concept of priestly office. The 'classical' doctrine begins with Church ministry and keeps this as its central point: Christ appointed office-bearers, Peter, the Apostles, the disciples, and gave them authority and power. In doing this, he founded the Church. The essential unity of the Church is consequently preserved by a visible authority, exercising a triple function — the authentic proclamation of the faith, the authorised celebration of the sacramental liturgy and pastoral ministry organised hierarchically. This authority is therefore the alpha and omega of the Church. This theological concept was cuttingly described by the great Tübingen scholar Johann Adam

Möhler as follows: 'God created the hierarchy, and that is enough provision for the Church until the end of the world.'

Canon law also was principally concerned with authority. Essentially only canon 682 spoke of the rights of the laity: 'The laity have the right to demand spiritual benefits, and, above all, helps to salvation, in accordance with Church discipline.' Since church authority represents Christ to the laity, the action and rights of the Church are to be attributed to its office-bearers.

About the time of the Second Vatican Council the pendulum swung in the opposite direction. Already before the Council, since about the end of the nineteenth century, various developments in the Church, such as the youth movement, the liturgical movement and above all Catholic Action, had led to an increasing realisation that the mission of Christ is not continued merely in the authorised ministry; consequently the Church is not built up by it alone: all Christians in virtue of their Baptism and Confirmation are commissioned to proclaim and bear witness to God's word and to work in spreading it; there is a common call to holiness, a common standing before God in praise, adoration and sacrifice. The Second Vatican Council drew the logical conclusion from this 'new' understanding of the Church. In its Constitution *Lumen gentium* it no longer defines the Church in terms of its governing authority, but, prior to all distinction of laity and ministry, describes it as the one people of God, in which all without exception are called 'to offer spiritual sacrifices and to proclaim the mighty deeds of the one who has called them out of the darkness into his marvellous light (cf. 1 Pet 2:4-10). Therefore, all disciples of Christ should persevere in prayer, praise God together (cf. Acts 2:42-47), and offer themselves as a living sacrifice, holy and pleasing to God. They must everywhere on earth bear witness to Christ and give an account to all who ask for it of the hope which they possess of eternal life (cf. 1 Pet 3:15)' (no. 10). Consequently there is also 'among them all a true equality in the dignity and in the activity common to all the faithful for the building up of the Body of Christ' (*Lumen gentium*, no. 32).

One must realise the tension which exists between these statements and the following statements — admittedly not voted on through lack of time — of Vatican I: 'The Church is not a community of members occupying equal positions in which all the faithful would have the same rights. It is a community of unequals, not only because some of the faithful are clergy and others laity, but also and principally because there is in the Church a divinely endowed authority — to sanctify, to teach and to guide; an authority which is granted to some of the faithful and not to others'. It is true that the Second Vatican Council also recognised a distinction based on particular vocation and mission between office-bearers and laity: but this distinction is part of the internal structure of the people of God, who are bound together in a shared dignity and mission. The apostolic duty of spreading the faith, the ministry of helping others, the celebration of the sacraments — all these take place in the Church as a whole, however differently all the members share in them according to their charismata, that is, their particular spiritual gifts.

But if the equality of all is stressed and if the common priesthood of all is emphasised in this way, what is then the *special* priesthood of the office-bearer, what further significance has priestly office? It is not surprising that the crisis of identity of priestly office begins just at this point. Cardinal Joseph Lefèbre, the archbishop of Bourges, speaking in the name of eighty French bishops, declared: 'In our days, when great importance is attached to the common priesthood of the baptised, and the apostolic action of the laity, many priests are bewildered.' The Council did in fact try to answer this difficulty as well (cf. *Lumen gentium*, no. 10), but it did not give a sufficiently clear solution for the problem thus posed. After the Council, the theologians took the matter up and in numerous studies and analyses — exegetical, dogmatic and historical — sought to determine the nature and centre of priestly office.

One widely accepted answer to this question about the distinctive feature of church authority runs roughly as follows: office is one charisma (a particular ability, ministry, function) among the many other charismata of the ecclesiastical community. Its distinctive mark is leadership of the community: that is, the special task of authority is to integrate, coordinate and stimulate the numerous other charismata, abilities, ministries and functions — to guide them towards unity, mutual interchange and service. In this way, authority is essentialy derived from the universal vocation of all the baptised to form part of the people of God. It is one ministry among the other abilities, ministries and duties *in* the Church.

Thus, church office is not in origin christological; that is, it is not derived from a special calling, commissioning and delegation by Christ which enables the office-bearer to represent him before the community. It is, rather, a way in which *the Church* represents itself and a way in which the life of the Church actually develops. It does not directly represent Christ, but specifically the Church, and only as a result of this does it represent Christ, the source and foundation of the Church and of its faith. It is primarily an office *of the Church*: it is an office *of Christ* only in so far as Christ is the Lord of the Church in which the priest holds office. Similarly the ministry of the priest is sacramental because the Church is sacramental in its nature and makes its sacramentality concrete and perceptible in the sacraments, including Holy Orders. In this way the ordination of a priest 'concentrates the priestly dimension of the Church in the person of the office-bearer, and makes the function, to which all are called — the proclamation and celebration of the mystery of Christ — explicit and public, in an organised and official manner' (L. Boff).

This approach to a theological explanation not only sets the ministry completely inside the community of baptised and confirmed Christians, but derives ministry entirely from the community. It results from a necessary swing of the pendulum away from an exaggerated pre-conciliar concept of ministry. It makes it clear that the people of God is the greater entity, because it includes both clergy and laity. It also becomes clear that the people of God and the charismatic gifts, ministries and duties which operate in it are not simply derived from church authority, and that consequently there exist a vocation and a claim on all believers issuing directly from the Spirit of God and not subject to the official Church. That is: any potentialities and activities which are found in the community are legitimated not only by church authority but by the sovereignty of the Spirit of God who works wherever he wishes, so that the office-bearer himself needs completion and correction through the spiritual gifts which are at work in the other baptised members. Last, but not least, this theological interpretation of ministry can illustrate the basic idea, already expressed in the Second Vatican Council, that ministry is above all a service to the community of the believers. The statement 'The charisma of ministry is a function on behalf of the other charismáta' is no more than a practical conclusion from this theological position.

What is meant here by the word 'function'? K. Rahner has illustrated it by the following comparison: 'priests are in a position similar to that of the officers of a chess club. Their functions cannot be undertaken by the individual players. But their functions have ultimately one purpose only — chessplaying of the highest class. The goal of the official priesthood is the priesthood of those who believe and love'. In accordance with this proposed interpretation, sacramental consecration — significantly the term 'ordination' is preferred — is primarily understood as an action of the Church, 'an official calling of a believer to the service of leadership, in which the Church recognises and endorses the calling from God. . . . It consequently results in spiritual legitimation for the community and for the ordained person himself' (H. Küng).

3. New questions and perspectives

All these statements can certainly be understood as being correct — but are they really exhaustive definitions of the essence of church authority and priestly consecration, or do they too not fall into onesidedness and because of their ambiguity produce misconceptions of authority analogous to those prevalent before the Council, but in the opposite direction?

To take but only example — the emphasis so popular now on the 'functional' aspect of authority. The concept of authority as a function of community leadership is frequently preferred to the concept of an interior vocation endowed with special power. But 'function' is an abstract concept, and if it is to be used concretely, it must be applied to the particular concrete situation. When the official Church 'functions', it is primarily a person who is 'functioning' inside a relationship which exists between Christ and his Church and which is essentially characterised by faith, hope and charity. If this 'functioning' is furthermore defined by a particular mission and witness in the context of the theological virtues — as we shall see later — the person who is 'functioning' is affected interiorly and essentially, since faith, hope and charity, mission and witness are interior realities which are very deeply personal.

These distinctions do not give a complete exposition of the concept of office as 'function', except as it is indiscriminately used today in controversial writings in opposition to the concept of office as an 'ontological' reality. But above all, this consideration shows that Rahner's comparison just cited (priest: official of a chess club) has no more than a very relative application. Above all, it cannot be understood to mean that church leaders have a merely extrinsic and pragmatic regulatory function in the 'real life' which goes on in the community (in which case why would it need leaders?). Since 'function' in the Church is interwoven with personal living of the faith and is carried out in the context of mission and witness, it is more than something purely external. It is necessary then to name this additional element and to explore its presuppositions and consequences. Furthermore, an exclusively functional view of church office cannot explain why it is that, in a community without a priest, one of the laity who possesses the human, theological and administrative qualifications for leadership does not become a holder of the priestly office, with all that that implies, by virtue of the fact that he has been appointed as a 'pastoral assistant' in that community and is accepted by it.

Thus, the statement 'Church office is a function, a leadership function in the Church' remains profoundly ambiguous.

Similarly ambiguous is the statement that church office does not originate primarily and directly from Christ, but from the Church which has produced it from itself as a necessary function.

This statement can firstly be understood as a purely empirical sociological one, which derives from the well-known fact that every pigeon-fanciers' club needs and appoints a governing committee. To put it more generally, every stable association, (including the Church) has a sociological need of a ruling group which it consequently evolves from itself and to which it appoints certain of its members. But if this is applied to the Church, the question still remains: What are the characteristic features of authority in that society which is an eschatological (= definitive and final) community of salvation, the people of God and body of Christ, and which points beyond itself in an unique manner, since it is willed by God as *his* work, is called by *him* and is empowered to receive and pass on *his* ultimate salvation. This absolute uniqueness of the Church, based on the eschatological promise of God, has consequences for all its institutions, and also for church office. As a result the generally valid empirical definition of authority is applicable to church office only in the broadest outline.

Alternatively, the interpretation of church office as a function can be strictly theological: the Church becomes 'concentrated' in the office, and this in such a way that, in it, what the Church is and how church life is passed on become obvious and palpable. Interpreted in this way the question still remains open: Has the ordained official a merely official responsibility for what is fundamentally the responsibility of the Church as a whole, or does ordination mean that some effect is produced by Christ on the ordained person (for the benefit of the Church, of course), an effect which the Church as a whole cannot confer and which is transmitted by Christ to the Church through the ordained person. If the latter is the case, then church office is not merely a function of the Church, not simply one charisma among the many gifts and vocations in the Church; on the contrary, because it is a special commission from Christ, it contrasts with the other charismata in a manner yet to be explained in detail.

From these and similar open questions and problems it is becoming increasingly clear in recent years that the 'new' theological approach which seeks to define Church office 'from below', that is, on the horizontal level of the various charismata in the Church, is inadequate. Nor is it enough to say that 'authority from below *is* actually authority from above' (E. Schillebeeckx), giving as a reason that calling and appointment by the Church, and the discharge of an ecclesiastical function, are 'the concrete ecclesial form of vocation from Christ' or are 'experienced as a gift of the Spirit, and thus as coming from above' (E. Schillebeeckx).

This identification of the action of the Church and the action of Christ, of what comes 'from below' and what comes 'from above', would be valid only if the Church and Christ were one and the same agent; if, that is, Christ had totally identified himself with the Church, and if the Church were totally identified with Christ. This mutual 'relationship of identity' is expressed, it is true, in the biblical image of the Church as the 'body of Christ' (1 Cor 12:12), and as the 'fulness' of Christ (Eph 4:13). But this is only *one* image of the reality of the Church. The Church is not merely the body of Christ, the fulness of him who fulfils all, but also the 'bride of Christ', who in her infinite need and poverty receives everything from him; it is the people of God, which he gathers together, the building which he builds. These images express an essential and even the most fundamental aspect of the Church: the Church owes everything to the Lord: its origin is not the spontaneous coming together of those who wish to be the people of God; it does not adopt its fundamental structure and form of life in a kind of vague spiritual enthusiasm; its journey and goal are not determined by human reflection or social contact. It is essentially the *ekklesia*, the community of those who are chosen, gathered and kept together by Jesus Christ, by his word and work. It is the *creatura Verbi*, created by the divine Word. It has, then, its foundation outside itself. This is not an incidental attribute of the Church, but the basic crucial datum of the faith.

Moreover, although Christ fills the Church with his life, and although the Church may venture to understand itself as his body, as the place, symbol and instrument (sacrament) of his presence, yet he is always antecedent to the Church, its Lord, Redeemer and 'Bridegroom', and the Church is always a creature, a 'charitable foundation', a needy bride who, while she is on her journey, remains ever inferior to the wealth of her Bridegroom. This distinction between Christ and the Church, which does not contradict their union, but instead emphasises the permanent gratuitousness and the present pilgrim nature of the Church, is fundamental for the Church's understanding of itself, and must consequently be applied in all church activity. An action of the Church ('from below') is never to be identified with the activity of Christ ('from above') in such a way that the necessary distinction between them is not simultaneously expressed: i.e., the distinction must appear in the symbol, since the Church is, in fact, a sacramental and symbolic reality which points to Christ and his salvation.

Where this distinction is overlooked, or is not recalled and demonstrated with sufficient clarity, there is the danger of a Church which in its basic activity does no more than celebrate its own unity, and which merely brings into play the abilities of its faithful (even though there be much talk of the Holy Spirit). The task of the official Church is to witness that Christ is and remains prior to his Church, and to make that priority effective in the centre of the Church's life — since it does not regard its office as derived *exclusively* from the community, or as one charisma among others, but as separate from them; in this way, with power given by Christ and symbolically pointing to him, church office makes the foundation of the Church, Christ himself, effectively present.

This ministry of authority does not of course stand apart from the church *communio*, mediating as it were between a 'distant' Christ and his Church: instead, it symbolically expresses and makes effective within that *communio* the basic distinctiveness of the Church's existence — the fact that Christ, living in the Church, himself calls and creates it.

For this reason vocation — and, above all, consecration — are necessary for church office. What this means is that its authority derives its legitimacy, not from an acquired competence, or from its own pretensions, or from a community producing it from within itself, but from the fact that Christ himself calls and consecrates and thus takes possession of a man, making him capable of 'representing' his reality in the Church — in word, in the celebration of the sacraments, in the service of leadership.

This representing is not to be understood in the modern sense of juridically authorised representation, but in a symbolical and sacramental sense — a 'making present' or, better, a real and effective appearance (even occurrence) of what is made present in symbol. The representative is strictly at the service of the reality represented by him. Ordination means much more than mere installation (with prayer and laying on of hands) in a post of public responsibility for discharging ecclesial duties: neither is it a purely juridical transfer of certain spiritual powers, nor can it be limited to 'the recognition of a charisma already present' (R. Sohm) or to simple appointment by the community (E. Schlink). It is much more: by his consecration (ordination) a man is 'dispossessed' of himself so that he can be 'a visible sign that the priestly work of the risen Lord is present' (F. Hahn).

Thus the people of God, entrusted to an office-bearer who is legitimated by consecration and who has a mission based on that consecration, experiences in a concrete manner the fact that it lives from the prior reality of Christ. Moreover, in this way the 'incarnational structure' of the whole transmission of salvation becomes clear. Salvation is not simply something spiritual which dissolves into subjectivity and thus is liable to distortion through subjective projections: on the contrary, it comes to men objectively, with a definite shape, sensible and corporeal, and as part of an institution — in a word, 'in the flesh'.

This concept of church office must in no way lead to a quasi-mystical identification of Christ and the office-bearer, although this misunderstanding was not always avoided in the past (for example, in the expression *sacerdos — alter Christus:* cf. p. 20). If one considers the strictly sacramental nature of church office, it will become clear that at the focal points of church life it is not a 'Father X' who is acting because he is particularly good, because he himself has acquired the competence to act or because the community have attributed this competence to him: on the contrary, it is because Christ has taken him into his service and legitimated him through consecration. It is this ordination that directs the community beyond the person of the office-bearer to Christ who has consecrated him. It is therefore not that a human authority is set up in place of Christ, but that Christ himself is effectively acting sacramentally, that is, in an effective sign through which he can be recognised and which directs attention to him. In this way the official authority of the priest is radically relative — directed away from himself and related to Christ and to the service of others.

This brief outline of the meaning of church office will be developed in greater detail in the next chapter:

In this chapter I may seem to be giving church office more prominence than the Church, advancing an out-of-date and inadequate pre-conciliar concept of the Church. This is not my intention. This impression may arise because, although theological teaching about church office should always be preceded by a detailed theological description of Church and community, this description for brevity's sake is not included here; it is taken for granted. What I have said also takes for granted the teaching of the Second Vatican Council about the Church as a community. According to the Council, the decisive structural element of the Church is not the existence of superiors and inferiors, that is, the distinction between clergy and laity, but the fraternal community of all Christians and the mutual service which they render to each other. 'Therefore, the chosen people of God is one. . . . From their rebirth in Christ they have a common dignity, a common grace as God's children, a common call to perfection; their salvation is one, one their hope and undivided their charity. Therefore, there are no inequalities in Christ and in the Church. . . . And if by the will of God some are constituted teachers, dispensers of the mysteries, and pastors of the others, yet there prevails among all a true equality in the dignity common to all the faithful and in their activity in building up the Body of Christ' (*Lumen gentium*, no. 32). From this starting-point, church office (and its special authority and mission) cannot be defined except as a service for fellow-Christians. Therefore, to define what the laity is, one must not begin with office: on the contrary, one must start with the laity, that is, with the community of the people of God, and then ask what is specific about the ministry (cf. p.18).

This specific element will be seen in the next chapter to consist firstly in the fact that office is representation of Christ. But this view of the ministry as being different from the other charismata is one-sided, in the truest meaning of the word. A proper balance is achieved only when, in the third chapter, ministry is seen as 'representation of the Church' and based on the action of the Spirit in the Church. Chapters Two and Three, therefore, consider church office from two points of view which are dialectically related to each other and are reconciled only in a trinitarian view of the work of salvation. To avoid misunderstanding this must be borne in mind when reading the individual chapters.

2

Ministry as a 'representation' of Christ: the christological foundation of ministry

1. Basic lines of the New Testament concept of ministry

If one's understanding of priestly office is not to be derived from personal arbitrariness and wilfulness, fashionable wishful thinking or sociological plausibility, if the 'minister of the Spirit' is not to become a 'minister of the spirit of the age' (J. M. Sailer), then all reflection on church office must be dependent on Holy Scripture and its living tradition. It must be measured and supported by the whole history of Christ and the original testimony borne of it. Certainly, one must also take into consideration that in recent years much research has been published on the New Testament origin of church office; and yet, as E. Schillebeeckx rightly remarks, many exegetical questions still remain unanswered. 'Historical reconstructions' of the structure of the New Testament communities and of the appointment, function and duties of their office-bearers (studies which claim to be complete and certain) go far beyond the narrow limits of this historical evidence — and are often developed to support a pre-conceived thesis.

Consequently, in what follows I make no attempt to 'reconstruct' the history of the development of a special ministry. Instead, what I will try to do is identify the persistent and unchanging theological circumstances and ideas which form the background of the New Testament concept of ministry.

a) *The mission of the disciples before the Resurrection* It may be taken as historically certain that Jesus in his lifetime gave men a share in his mission of service for the kingdom of God which was already dawning (cf. e.g. Mk 3:13f; 6:6-13). This means that the disciples were to do fully and completely all that Jesus himself was doing. Like him they were to announce the approach of the kingdom and to perform the signs of the kingdom: 'Heal the sick, raise the dead, cleanse the lepers, drive out demons!' (Mt 10:8). Even in their lifestyle (poverty, availability, commitment) they were to resemble him: they were not only messengers, but authorised witnesses, fellow-workers, 'representatives' of Jesus. Their witness and authority were not based on a kind of juridical authorisation but on a mission which prescribed a pattern for their whole manner of life, since it was derived from their personal union with Jesus. Since they belonged 'to him', they could and should effectively carry him and his cause to where he wished to come (cf. Lk 10:1). When after the Resurrection this authority was understood in the Church as conferring the power to bind and loose, enabling the disciples to act effectively in God's sight and to adjudicate on salvation and judgment (Mt 18:18), or when their mission was explained as a continuation of the mission given to Jesus by the Father ('As the Father has sent me, I also send you': Jn 20:21), it was only the development of something already contained in principle in the disciples' pre-Resurrection mission. It is true that that mission did not continue, without a break, into the official mission of the Apostles after the Resurrection. There is nevertheless a basic continuity which is easily overlooked if the pre-Resurrection mission of the disciples is described as an 'eschatological testimony' and is set apart from later apostolic or even priestly office. In each there was a mission of witness given by the Lord: in each the one sent stood (in his being and activity) for the one who sent him. The difference between the two missions arises from the difference in the 'eschatological situation' in which each mission was given. In the earthly lifetime of Jesus, the disciples were commissioned to announce the imminent approach of the kingdom of God in word and visible signs of power: after the Resurrection they were witnessing to the beginning of the kingdom which had already come about through the death of Jesus.

Through the Resurrection of Christ and the sending of the Holy Spirit the kingdom had irrevocably come to the world — admittedly in a preliminary and partially developed form which would be completed in the future. But the power of death and sin *was* broken, and the covenant between God and man *was* ratified for ever, the Spirit of the last age *was already* making a new life possible; what concerns the world to come and life eternal was already anticipated in the Christian community (E. Käsemann). With the Resurrection of Christ the kingdom of God of the last age had begun, and consequently the original office of 'eschatological' witness was no longer only a duty to proclaim something which was to come. It was now a comprehensive ministry of the means of salvation for the world, and especially for that community whose whole life is derived from the coming of the kingdom — the people of God. The ultimate basis of the mission remains the same: just as the pre-Resurrection mission of the disciples was rooted in their being sent by Jesus, so also apostolic office corresponds to a particular commission from the Lord.

b) *Paul as an example of apostolic ministry* This becomes particularly clear from the manner in which the Apostle Paul (who in the early Church was already regarded as *the* Apostle) viewed and practised his ministry. Just as in the account of the calling of the disciples by Jesus it is said that those were called 'whom *he* chose' (Mk 3:13), so also Paul regards himself as called to his ministry by Jesus Christ, in fact by God himself, and not by the community (cf. 1 Cor 1:1;2 Cor 1:1). 'Paul, called to be an Apostle, not by men or through a man, but by Jesus Christ and by God the Father, who raised him from the dead' (Gal 1:1). His view of his ministry is especially clear in a passage from the second epistle to the Corinthians (2 Cor 5:14 - 6:1).

[14]The love of Christ constrains us when we reflect that if one man died for all, then all died. [15]But he died for all so that those who live should no longer live for themselves, but for him who died and was raised to life for them. . . . [17]If therefore anyone is in Christ, he is a new creation: the old (covenant) is gone, and a new one is now here. [18]All this comes from God who reconciled us to himself through Christ and charged us with the ministry of reconciliation. [19]Indeed it was God who in Christ is reconciling the world to himself, not imputing to men their sins and entrusting to us (the preaching of) the work of reconciliation. [20]We are therefore ambassadors for Christ, and it is God who is warning through us: we appeal in Christ's name: be reconciled to God! . . . . [1]As fellow-workers [of God] we exhort you not to receive the grace of God in vain.

Even the general context of this important passage is significant. In 2 Corinthians Paul had to justify to the community his apostolic office of proclaiming the Gospel, an office which he understands as a *diakonia pneumatos*, a ministry of the Spirit (3:8). The starting point of his argument, in the passage just quoted, is the salvation which has been accomplished in Jesus Christ. Paul is impressed by the love of Christ (v.14), which men can recognise in his acceptance of death and in his Resurrection. In this passage he is speaking about the central element of the Christian faith, the death and Resurrection of Jesus Christ. Through the risen Lord the old (covenant) has passed away and all is now new (v.17). In v.18 the ultimate author of the achievement of salvation (God the Father) and the inmost core of Christ's work (reconciliation) are named and then concisely expressed: 'He has reconciled us to himself through Christ *and* charged us with the ministry of reconciliation'. Thus at a decisive point, where Paul is describing the central doctrine of the Christian faith, he speaks in the same breath of the ultimate foundation and basic essence of his apostolic office: by the decisive salvific act of reconciliation, God has at the same time and by the same act instituted the ministry of reconciliation. In the act of reconciliation through the cross of Christ, God has accomplished a twofold effect in one action: he has reconciled us to himself through Christ *and* instituted the ministry of reconciliation. Both are joined together in the closest manner possible. Church office is therefore 'not something which was introduced later, due perhaps to human missionary initiative' (E. Dinkler); no, it was established with and in the saving work of Cross and Resurrection.

Verse 19 resumes v.18 in a new formulation. Paul points out emphatically that God the Father is the reconciler, but that he accomplishes the reconciliation in and through Jesus Christ. And once again, God's salvific act in and through Jesus Christ *and* the institution of the corresponding office are seen together as one single event. The one act of God gives both salvation (not imputing sins) and also the ministry of salvation commissioned with it. They are inseparably connected. Consequently Paul can in v.20 sum up his concept of his office: 'We are therefore ambassadors for Christ!': and this amounts to saying 'It is God who is warning through us' (v.20b). This claim is repeated once again as if it could not be said often enough: 'We ask you on behalf of Christ!'. 'Thus it is emphasised three times that God (or Christ) is the one who summons, invites and calls, that the proclamation of the Gospel does not derive from the insight and wisdom of the Apostle. In the call which follows, it is God who is present, it is really Christ who invites: the Apostle is the ambassador of his Lord. Because he is authorised in this way, the word he speaks is the word of God and Christ: he is only the mouthpiece and not the originator of the message when he calls, "Be reconciled with God!" . . . The call itself is therefore a summons to accept what God has done in and through Christ, to accept God's offer and accomplishment of salvation, which has come about antecedently to all human action and conduct' (E. Dinkler). God the Father is consequently the ultimate author of the work of salvation; nevertheless, his action is carried out through Christ and in Christ *and* through the medium of the official Church, that is through and in those who are specially authorised. These are, therefore, in a proper sense fellow-workers of God. This is exactly what is expressly said in 1 Cor 6:1: 'as fellow-workers of God, we admonish you . . .'.

The message of reconciliation, which is entrusted to the fellow-worker, must not be understood as merely preaching 'about' salvation. In biblical usage *logos* includes the reality which it denotes. Thus the 'word of reconciliation' means not only the preaching of the Good News, but also the reality of the Gospel itself, a reality which is promised and effected. The authority set up with the act of salvation has therefore the task of spreading the reconciliation already been brought about by God in Jesus Christ, to make it effectively present to all mankind and at all times. This transmission is effected in an extremely concrete manner, above all through the forgiving and consoling, appealing and encouraging message of the Gospel, and through founding and leading communities which give a preview of the new world of God as 'a city set on a hill' (Mt 5:14), that is, 'the ideal society of God' (N. Lohfink), a pre-vision of God's new world of justice and love, communication and mutual assistance, joy and peace.

Those engaged in this ministry of transmitting salvation are not acting from their own abilities. They are men authorised and charged to 'represent Christ'. This expression is biblical, but it is liable to be misunderstood. It can be taken as implying that Christ needs a representative because he is absent. But this would be absurd. The Lord is present in his Church, and the authority set up simultaneously with his work of salvation must not replace immediate relationship to him: instead it must actually make that relationship possible. Thus, church office represents Christ himself, that is, makes him present in sign, word and action, and causes him to appear himself, since it is a sacrament, an effective sign of him through which he can be seen. To take an (inadequate) comparison: the window of a room does not prevent contact between the world outside and inside the room; it actually produces that contact. Similarly, the transmission of salvation through the official Church does not destroy the immediacy of contact with Christ, but opens the way to it. This sacramental relation of Christ and church office is analogous to the relationship of God (the Father) to Jesus Christ. Jesus Christ is the representative of the Father: 'He who sees me, sees the Father' (Jn 14:9). But his revelation is not made by him instead of by the Father, replacing immediate contact with the Father; his activity is, rather, a revelation of his cooperation with the Father, who is present in him. For 'the Father who abides in me' does the works which Jesus does (Jn 14:10). Jesus is not stationed between mankind and the Father: he *is*, rather, the visible immediacy of the Father, and in him men are in immediate contact with the Father. In a similar way the person entrusted with the ministry of reconciliation does not 'replace' the absent Lord; instead the Lord himself makes room for men to work with him for others. Thus, the 'representation of Christ by the official Church is not a way of saying that Christ has departed from the Church; but that on the contrary he continues his work to the end by means of the office-bearers who represent him' (P. E. Persson). The cooperation of Christ's commissioned fellow-workers consists in this, that they make God visible and audible, that they are a sacrament of him and make sacramentally present — that is, sacramentally represent — the God who wills to accomplish the work of salvation. Consequently they do not stand in God's way but are instead the way (or, better, a way) in which his salvific action reaches mankind. They are thus not an intermediate stage between God (Christ) and the community, but on account of the double relationship in which they stand (taken into service *by God — for the others*) they effect a (mediated) immediacy. Therefore, those who receive salvation are indeed dependent on the sacramental mediation of the official Church, but not in such a way that they are cut off from God and in contact with his representative without being united with God. On the contrary, in the sacramental mediation they meet God himself in his self-revelation to the world.

Church office is part of the manner in which God communicates with men. V. Campenhausen rightly remarks that 'All human "fellow-workers with God" can for their part only help to effect this decisive immediate contact: they belong to the community, not the community to them. . . . In the community, the Apostle stands for Christ, not in the way of Christ.' This is precisely the reason why for Paul the powerlessness of the official Church, the failure of the official minister, the weakness of the preacher, the inadequacy of his mode of speech are . . . irrelevant ' (E. Dinkler). It is not the Apostle who has the ability to communicate salvation to men: the effectiveness of his activity comes wholly from God (2 Cor 3:5); it is God's strength in human weakness (2 Cor 12:9-10). Paul, therefore, criticises Christians who demand personal qualification as a legitimation of his ministry — qualifications such as the gift of tongues from the Spirit, charismatic powers, power to work miracles, ecstasies. His legitimation is his calling and mission through Christ: nothing else. On the contrary, anyone who claims to be of himself capable of holding apostolic office, and who points to his personal talent for it, is like a 'seller in the marketplace' who is hawking his own wares (cf. 2 Cor 2:17). Merchants of this kind subject the Gospel to the 'variation of supply and demand. But in this they betray the fact that they are not concerned about the truth of their cause. It is subjected to other, irrelevant criteria, the laws of the marketplace' (D. Georgi). One who pushes himself forward, is pushing aside what is essential — namely that it is God himself who offers reconciliation and salvation through the Apostle, who is the medium through whom God is immediately present, binding the believer to himself (and not to the official Church).

The assertion of H. Schleier may be onesided and exaggerated: 'The Apostle never regards himself as an interpreter for his communities, but always . . . as their "partner", essentially allied with them'; but it is true that for Paul 'the institution of the office of proclamation is God's action'; it is part 'of the whole process of salvation', and therefore 'of that gift of grace which comes from

God'(E. Dinkler). Consequently, in this dependence on church office, the Church and the individual believer realise through a sacramental sign the priority of the operation of grace and of the authority of Jesus Christ. In this sense also the Apostle is distinct from the community and exercises his ministry by a special commission from the Lord, acting together with him as his 'representative' and as his (sacramental) 'vicegerent'.

c) *Paul and the community* All the Pauline epistles which have come down to us bear witness to the fact that Paul did this and to the way in which he did it. Even though he exercised his office charismatically, i.e. in the power and ability conferred by the Spirit, he nevertheless distinguishes his official apostolic activity from all actions of the community, no matter how much they may come from spiritual charismata. He speaks with authority in the name of the Kyrios (2 Cor 13:3) and gives instructions with the full authority which he possesses. He claims the right to test and regulate charismata, and to do this 'in virtue of his power of maintaining law and order in the Church' (E. Käsemann). All his letters give evidence of this: 'Paul begs and advises, encourages and warns, but he also demands and threatens, upbraids them and puts them to shame, is merciful and corrects them, gives strict orders and regulations, forbids and punishes. Certainly the authoritative and peremptory element should not be overemphasised (cf. 2 Cor 1:24; 8:8); but neither should one suppress it and reduce the instructions of the Apostle to tactful recommendations and good advice' (W. Schrage). Paul knows that he has a specific apostolic *exousia* (= authority) which he can use and in virtue of which he can compel obedience. Through this *exousia* he makes regulations for ordering the gifts of the Spirit. Anyone of the *pneumatici* who does not acknowledge this fact will not be acknowledged himself by God at the Last Judgment. It is certainly no accident that Paul exercises and defends this apostolic authority of his with the 'charismatic' community of Corinth in particular. To it he can write the angry words, 'If someone thinks that he is a prophet or filled with the Spirit, he should recognise that what I write to you is a command of the Lord. He who does not recognise this, will not be recognised' (1 Cor 14:37). In other words: the charismatic gift of the Spirit is proved precisely by the agreement of its possessor with the authoritative directions the Apostle gives.

In recent years not a few pronouncements on the theology of church office have put forward the community of Corinth as a model of the concept of church and authority for the future. In Corinth, it is said, there was no office-bearer in the strict sense, but a multitude of different charismata, each of which contributed what was lacking in the others. These charismata were ministries filled with the Spirit and their authority was founded on the verified power of the Spirit, not on formal and official appointment and mission.

Against this, however, it must be said that this picture of the community of Corinth hardly corresponds with reality. It cannot be denied that already in the lifetime of the Apostles and under their supervision there were leaders of local communities, who had a share in the apostolic powers. Together with the Apostles and unlike the rest of the faithful they were 'fellow-workers of God' (1 Cor 3:9). This is true of the Pauline communities in particular. If this situation is not expressly stated in the letters to the Corinthians, it must be remembered that the problem in the Corinthian community was a problem of unity: the community was in danger of breaking up on account of the multitude of different charismata. Paul, therefore, insists precisely on this point, that the great abundance and variety of the gifts of the Spirit must, in spite of their difference, be combined to form a unity. Thus, the situation led to particular emphasis on charismata and can therefore give the impression that the church order at Corinth did not include a particular authority or particular authorities. But since the actual situation in the other Pauline communities is described differently, it seems that the picture of a purely charismatic community in Corinth is unhistorical.

Moreover, it is usually not noticed that Paul was setting the full authority of his ministry over against a community that prided itself on its charismata. Just because the Apostle himself was accessible, being present in person or through messengers or letters (in these cases the letter or messenger 'represented' the Apostle himself), it was also not necessary in his lifetime for the structures of authority in the local community to be laid down in the last detail. This necessity first arose after the death of the Apostles.

Thus the remark of Harnack (against Sohm) is still valid: 'It cannot be conceded that the character of an organisation, even a specifically charismatic one, can remain based on charisma — even for a short while only, let alone in its development through time. That would only be the case if there were only prophecies but no prophets, teachings but no teachers, directions but no leaders: everything would happen by fits and starts. But it has never been so and can never be so.'

Finally, with regard to the model character of the Corinth community asserted by many theologians today, one must argue together with A. Müller: 'if charismatic church structures are put forward against a theological explanation of authority, in the name of enlightened theology, this is open to the accusation of irrationality. It is irrational to demand direct manifestation of the Spirit as proof of a charisma and to play it off against rational structures. And it is irrational (inasmuch as one fails to recognise anthropological facts) if one simply denies sociological development to a group or a movement and leaves it fixed in an original group-situation, as if a fleeting charismatic experience was enough to hold the group permanently together .

One thing is certain: Paul is exercising in relation to the community an authority passed on to him by the Lord. Indeed the Evangelical theologian H. v. Compenhausen actually thinks — in my view he exaggerates — that it must be expressed as follows: Paul stands 'above the community. He is not inserted in it as a "member" but through an immediate call by Christ he has, as it were, a source peculiar to himself. But the prophets and also the teachers and all other men of the Spirit stand fully inside the community, and consequently remain bound by the testimony which they have received from the Apostle'.

Certainly Paul refrains whenever possible from authoritative intervention in the life of the community and prefers to work by way of requests and admonitions. He prefers to come to them 'in love and a spirit of mildness' instead of 'with a rod' (1 Cor 4:21). He does not order Philemon, but appeals to him 'for love's sake' (Philem 8). To the Thessalonians, instead of standing on his authority as an Apostle, he is as 'a nursing mother who cherishes her children' (1 Thess 2:7). But this does not take from his fundamental authority.

The same is true of the relation of apostolic office to the other charismata. Paul can in fact also set his ministry beside the other ministries and missions in the community (cf. 1 Cor 12:28). He exercises his apostolic mission amid many other missions and ministries (which he urges are to be recognised and respected: cf.1 Thess 5:12ff; 1 Cor 16:15ff). He is, therefore, not the only point of reference in the community and not the only 'instrument' through which Christ acts. Nevertheless, as the 'servant of Christ and steward of the mysteries of God' (1 Cor 4:1) he has been entrusted by the Lord himself with special and unique task — to 'represent' him (= to make him present) (cf. p. 28 above) and to maintain unity in the community. Of course, not merely in the community! The Apostle is at the same time the bond of unity between many communities, through communication in faith, through his journeys and letters, through mutual help and not least through prayers for one another.

Although his special authority is clear throughout, it is nevertheless fundamentally and essentially limited by the fact that it is not his own authority which appears in him, but that of the Lord. The communities do not belong to the Apostle and are not subject to *him*; they belong to Christ himself and obey the Lord, who is 'represented' in the Apostle.

For the correct evaluation of apostolic authority it is necessary to realise that as an individual the Apostle is, like all others, dependent on the salvific action of Christ. So he appears — as E. Schlink has appositely expressed it — 'as the greatest of sinners in his own estimation, as one born out of due time, as an excrescence, as a doormat, as least worthy, as one stricken by demons. . . . The Apostle stands as a witness before the community and brings everything to it — and at the same time it is true that he stands under the Lord as a pardoned sinner and is nothing before him. Thus, like every Christian, the Apostles supported by the assurance of consolation from the community. Their life is supported by the intercessions of the community: again and again we read how Paul begs them to pray for him, to pray that his work may go forward, that his sadness be taken from him, etc. Thus, the life of the Apostles is supported by the help of the community. They are dependent, not merely on material gifts and services, but also on the spiritual gifts of strength and consolation which the communities provide for them.'

Although the Apostle is bound up in this way with the whole people of God, he nevertheless possesses a special authority. It is an authority of service in two senses of the word. 1. It is a service to Christ. Therefore, Paul ventures to speak only about what Christ gives him to say (Rom 15:18), and he knows that he must render an account to Christ (1 Cor 4:4ff). 2. It is a service to the community. Therefore, he does not speak as the lord of the community's faith but as a fellow-worker for their joy (2 Cor 1:24).

Indeeed it is to be noted that the slogan 'Not domination but service!", applying a crude concept of domination to the official Church, rests on alternatives not derived from the New Testament. 'One who has authority is thereby able and on occasion obliged to use it. What matters is how it is used. The well-known pertinent warnings of Jesus do not mean that authority may never be exercised among the disciples, but that it must not be exercised after the manner of pagan rulers' (B. Beilner). If Christ was and is the Lord of his disciples, there must also be in the Church an authority which makes him present and in which he may be recognised. It must, of course, be exercised as he exercised it — as a selfless fraternal pastoral service to others.

In the apostolic ministry we can see the original form of all church authority — making allowances for all the modifications to be considered later. The proof of this assertion will be given after the 'priestly' character of apostolic office has been considered.

d) *The priestly character of apostolic office* The word 'priest' is actually derived from the Greek word *presbyteros* (= elder) and consequently had at first no connotation of religious cult. In the course of time, however, the meaning and significance of church office gradually extended to include the liturgical and sacramental sphere. As a result, its culmination, integrating all else, was taken to be the sacramental liturgy (especially the Eurcharist) and the priest was regarded as a sacerdotal intermediary of salvation between God and man.

This restricted view has been widened by the Second Vatican Council. The Council took up the concept current in Reformed theology (and adopted even before the Council by Catholic theologians) that Jesus Christ himself has a triple office: Christ is Prophet and teacher; he is Pastor and leader, and he is Priest — all three in an inseparable unity. If then, as we have seen, the official Church represents Christ, this is also under the triple aspect of teaching, leading and priestly sanctification: all three belong inseparably to the ministry of the official Church. These tasks open up the narrow concept of a priesthood restricted to the priestly functions of religious cult and place it in the totality of the mission of Christ and the Apostles. Nevertheless, the fact remains that the sacerdotal element is in fact a part — even if one among others — of the Catholic understanding of church office. Does this find support in the apostolic ministry? Is it not remarkable, and a relevant criterion, that nowhere in the New Testament is the word *hiereus* (= priest) applied to an Apostle or any other office-bearer? It is not said of any office-holder of apostolic or subapostolic times that he had a special authority or responsibility for divine worship. Moreover, is it not expressly stated that the priesthood of Jesus Christ brought all human priesthood to an end? Has not every Christian immediate access to God, so that there is no longer any need of sacerdotal mediation? In fact, does not such an office, particularly when organised as a hierarchy, only infringe on Christian liberty and lead away from the one essential cult — the Christian ministry to the world?

We have already seen that apostolic office is founded by Christ; it is in essence a 'representative' continuation of his mission by authorised ambassadors. Consequently, there can be no other priesthood in the Church than the sacramental representation of his unique and definitive priesthood.

What does that mean? Firstly, in the Old Testament, (above all in the earliest layers) priesthood is placed in a context wider than that of cult and sacrifice: the priest is above all the 'man of God', who is specially near to God and is called and empowered by him to give others access to God in many different ways. The marks of this 'priesthood' are very great nearness to God and very great activity for the salvation of all men. From this point of view Jesus Christ is already simply *the* priest. *Besides this,* however, Holy Scripture applies to Christ the concept of priest in the narrow cultic sense as well. In this sense the priesthood of Christ has fulfilled and abrogated every human 'cult': for his priesthood was of an entirely special kind. He was a priest precisely because he offered *himself* as a victim, and thus wrought satisfaction and salvation and instituted the New and definitive Covenant of God with man. It is true that this is expressly reflected only in the epistle to the Hebrews (9:11ff), but the reality of it is found in many places in the New Testament, above all where Jesus' offering of himself for our sake is spoken of, e.g. Eph 5:2: 'Christ loved us and gave himself up for us, an offering and a sacrifice pleasing to God'. His sacrifice reached its highest point in his death on the cross, but it encompassed his entire life: for it is true of his whole life that he was obedient unto death, even to the death of the cross (cf. Phil 2:8). Thus, all the activity of Jesus, his preaching and healing, consoling and leading, bore the stamp of devotion to God, because it was aimed solely at preparing a people which would go with him to the Father along the road of self-sacrifice. Consequently, the 'priestly' ministry of Jesus consists in 'the sacrificial service of obedient self-surrender to God for the sake of men ... in other words, the priesthood of Christ is to be distinguished but not to be separated from his office of prophet and pastor' (H. Schlier).

That a priest should go before God with his own blood (cf. Heb 9:12), making priestly ministry a self-offering, is a *paradox* which completely transforms and even breaks down the earlier concept of priesthood, with the result that one can call Christ a priest only if one goes on to explain what one means. His is a priesthood of a new and unique kind, in which all other human priesthood is taken away, and yet elevated and preserved. Therefore, there can be no other independent priesthood beside him and after him: all there can be is sacramental representation of his priesthood, allowing it to produce its effect.

From this point of view, it is a mistake in method to begin with a general concept of priesthood derived from the history of religion, a concept characterised by cult-sacrifice, and then to go on to ask if it is valid for the ministry which the Apostles had. If this were to be done, the only conclusion could be: 'Paul does not regard himself ... as a priest: on the contrary he abrogates all that is priestly since he reduces it to a metaphor for his "unpriestly activity"' (W. Pesch). But this 'unpriestliness' is precisely what brings all priesthood to fulfilment in Jesus Christ; it is not a matter of a cultic offering by a priest: it is the offering of self to God which is accomplished in Christ. In the apostolic ministry this offering must reach to all times and places as an opportunity and invitation, enabling and challenging all men and women — each according to his or her own vocation but united with the others — to follow along the way of the self-sacrifice of Christ.

There are indications that Paul himself understood his commission to preach the message of reconciliation as a priestly activity. In 1 Cor 9:13ff the ministry of the Gospel is placed in strict parallelism with the Old Testament service of the altar. The Gospel proclamation of the sacrifice of Jesus and the challenge to enter into his sacrifice (Rom 12:1; 6:19 and frequently) are, as it were, the new 'priestly office'. Paul describes it in this way: 'God has given me the grace to labour as a minister (*leitourgos*) of Christ Jesus to the Gentiles, ministering as a priest the Gospel of God: that the Gentiles may become an offering pleasing to God and sanctified in the Holy Spirit' (Rom 15, 16). Similarly in Phil 2:17: 'Even if I am being poured out as a drink offering together with the sacrifice and divine service of your faith, I rejoice and share my joy with you all.' Consequently, Paul understood his apostolic activity to be a 'a public and official sacrifice - *leitourgia* for the whole world' (H. Schlier).

Of course, this may be regarded as an image or metaphor. But it is not only an image.[2] 'For Paul the proclamation of the Gospel has taken the place of the sacrifices of the Old Testament, and hence of every sacrifice. For the Apostle, priestly work has been absorbed into the Apostolate, which is a ministry of the Gospel.' By the apostolic preaching, the self-offering of Jesus for the world is made present; it comes before us 'in the form of the word.' Indeed, it can be said that in Apostolic preaching the Lord himself causes us to come in contact with his sacrifice and in it with himself 'in the form of the word.' Thus, the priesthood of Jesus Christ 'is effectively mediated in the priestly ministry of the Gospel' (H. Schlier). Consequently apostolic office can be called 'priestly': not because it has responsibility for cult or because it offers 'sacrifice', but because it testifies to the self-sacrifice of Jesus for us, making this sacrifice present for us as a gift and as a task to be performed by us, and because it founds amd leads local communities according to this 'programme'.

The fact that the word 'priest' and related expressions are used in the New Testament with great discretion, and that (except in the epistle to the Hebrews) the word itself is not used in reference to Christ or the ministers of the Church, can be explained by the Church's need, in the first phase of its life, to distinguish itself clearly from Judaism and the Jewish cult. However, once it was realised that the New Testament was the completion of the pre-Christian order of salvation, a great influx of priestly terminology came into the Church. Moreover, the Church was forcing its way into a pagan milieu, in which the title of High Priest indicated high social rank. (Both these developments occurred about the time of Cyprian.)

e) *A priestly people and priestly office* What has been asserted so far about apostolic office and its priestly character was not attributed exclusively to the apostle himself, but also to the Twelve together with Paul, the 'additional' Apostle. Is it not perhaps true as well of the other witnesses of the Resurrection?

The Apostles, it is true, were given special authority by the Lord himself: they had therefore an 'origin' of their own and were ranked before the communities: it was in fact through their ministry that the people of God was first established. They are, therefore, the permanent foundation of the Church. But, when the Apostles had died and after local churches had been founded by them, did not their special function then pass on to the people of God as a whole, so that — on the foundation of the Apostles — *either* 'all the baptised' were now 'office-bearers' *or* special authorities were now set up from within the Church? Does this not fit in with the simple observed fact that the post-apostolic office-bearer arises from an already existing local community, since he receives his faith from the Church, and is ordained and commissioned by the Church? Looked at in this way, the structure of the post-apostolic ministry would be different from that of the apostolic Church, since 'it essentially develops from the mystery of the priestly Church' (F. Wulf). The post-apostolic ministry would have no origin of its own, rooted in Christ himself, and would no longer be distinguished from the community through being derived from Christ. Instead, it would be shown to be ultimately a (delegated) function of the community itself. The question therefore arises: Without affecting the unique and unrepeatable position of the Apostles, does authority in the Church continue without a break from the apostolic office? Has it its origin not only in the community but also in Jesus Christ, in virtue of a special mission and grant of power? Does it, therefore, receive its credentials and role not from the Church, but from the Lord himself?

At first sight it could appear that the priestly-apostolic ministry devolves upon the community *as a whole*. Some central passages of Scripture speak of the priesthood of the entire covenant people of the New Testament: Christ has acquired a people of priests. Thus in Rev 1:5: 'He loves us and delivered us from our sins through his blood; he made us to be kings and priests before his God and Father.' This 'priesthood' means, above all, that the redeemed are constantly offering to God through Christ 'the sacrifice of praise, that is the fruit of the lips that praise his name' (Heb 13:15). The promise of God is also the central feature in the text of the first epistle of Peter (1:2, 9), 'You are a chosen race, a royal priesthood, a holy nation, a people that has become his own possession, that you may proclaim the great deeds of him who has called you out of darkness into his wondrous light.' The *eucharistia* which Christ himself offered to the Father broadens out, as it were, in the *eucharistia* of the people and becomes a present reality in the many brothers and sisters of Christ. This priestly liturgy of the whole people of God is not restricted to praise and adoration: it is intended to include the whole of life. This is what constitutes the 'true service of God' — to offer oneself to the Father in all areas of one's life as 'a living and holy sacrifice' (cf. Rom 12:1). It is a sacrifice which is accomplished in mutual service, in help and love, and it is perfected in witness through suffering (martyrdom) with Christ and for Christ. For this very reason the martyrs particularly were called 'priests of God and of Christ' (Rev 20:6).[3]

Regarded in this way, the priestly mission of Jesus passes over to the whole people of God, which becomes a priestly people. The early theology of the Church was fully conscious of this. Consequently, the Second Vatican Council could link up not only with Holy Scripture but also with a long tradition when it emphasised that in Christ 'all the faithful become a holy and royal priesthood: they offer spiritual sacrifices to God through Jesus Christ, and proclaim the mighty deeds of the one who has called them out of darkness into his wonderful light. Thus there is no member who has no share in the mission of the whole body' (*Presbyterorum ordinis*, no. 2). All are 'made into the people of God, and are in their own way given a share in the priestly, prophetic and royal office; they carry out in their own way the mission of the whole Christian people in the Church and in the world' (*Lumen gentium*, no. 31).

This 'priesthood of all the faithful' does not, however, mean the exclusion of a special priestly office or its limitation. For this there are two decisive reasons:

1. The universal priesthood does not mean that each individual is 'his own priest': it is rather to be understood as strictly collective. It primarily refers to the people of God as a whole, and to the individual only to the extent that he belongs to this people. The expression 'priestly people' is a title of honour belonging to Israel, which is passed on to the New Testament community. This title does not express a permanent or temporary office of any kind: it is a call to the Church to live as a people sanctified for God in the same way as Israel was called. This means that it is priestly because the chosen people is specially and intimately close to God and belongs to him, through its 'priestly vocation' to praise God and through its 'priestly attitude' of sacrificial service in and for the world. In this way the community of the baptised is drawn into the (priestly) activity of Jesus for others.

2. The priestly character of the whole people of God does not exclude but includes a sacramental differentiation in its inmost being and way of life. Membership of the people of God, the devotion of all to the Father, and service to the world are only possible through Jesus Christ: they involve a continuous union with him in being and in action.

But Christ communicates *himself*, his word and the gifts of his Spirit to us 'sacramentally', that is, in signs which he uses and to which he gives power, signs which point to his person and 'represent' him, produce his effective presence. Among these mediating signs apostolic office is primary and essential. In it the permanent priority of Christ to the people of God is continued and becomes the permanent foundation of the Church. This apostolic foundation, incorporated in the Church and serving as its foundation, needed personal office-bearers after the end of the apostolic age. For the foundation is certainly not some indeterminate intangible entity: it takes shape in persons authorised to testify. Thus we find already in the authentic Pauline epistles a structure, a blueprint, according to which the Apostle with his authority is present in the local churches not only by means of his letters but also through his messengers and fellow-workers. The pastoral epistles link up without a gap with this structure. The Apostle, and consequently the apostolic tradition, are effectively present in the post-apostolic official Church. For this reason the post-apostolic office-bearers should 'like the Apostles (1 Cor 4:1; Rom 10:14 — 15:17) stand in the name of Christ and in his service' (Schillebeeckx). They, like the Apostles, are his 'representatives'.

The new feature of ministry in the post-apostolic period is that it sees itself as structurally connected with the apostolic heritage: through the post-apostolic office the Church was to be preserved in the apostolicity derived from the Apostles. Consequently, it can in a way be said that, in the post-apostolic ministry, the individual believer encounters the bond which holds the whole church community together, and the foundation upon which it rests — 'apostolicity'. 'In the official Church, the community is "represented" in a form which the individual can see and perceive; now it becomes evident that the Church . . . is more than the sum of the individual believers, and is really prior to them, and that it can come in a concrete form to the individual with its gifts and with its demands. . . . For this reason the faith of the individual is changed from being an act which is quite free and subjectively arbitrary, and is shaped and fitted into the larger *communio* of the faith' (M. Kehl). Certainly, in this sense church office would be only an office of the Church: it would show that the Church built on the foundation of the Apostles is prior to the individual member. But as we have already seen the apostolic foundation is in reality the continuation of the absolute priority of Christ himself (he is prior not only to the individual but also to the whole Church). To this extent, those who represent the priority of the Apostles are also in a much deeper sense representatives and ambassadors of Christ, and consequently have a double relationship — to the apostolic foundation of the Church and to the Lord who through their ordination commissions and empowers them.

The fact that the post-apostolic ministry is also derived from Christ is expressed in a series of New Testament texts. Thus, e.g., Eph 4:11 connects the founding of the original apostolic ministry by Christ with the post-apostolic pastoral and teaching ministry: 'and he gave to some the office of apostles, he appointed others as prophets, others as evangelists, others as pastors and teachers, in order to equip the saints for fulfilling their service in the building up of the body of Christ.' Therefore, it is Christ himself who has also by setting up the post-apostolic ministries built up his 'body', i.e. his own fulness in the history of salvation. At the same time this text states the central purpose of the post-apostolic ministry: the permanent foundation was laid by the witness of the Apostles, but the 'building up' of the priestly people of God goes on, and does so in the same way as the laying of the apostolic foundation — through authorised messengers, who as 'fellow-workers of God' must see to it that the brethren can perform their service, that God's field may bear fruit, that his 'building' may be completed (1 Cor 3:9). In the same way, in the first (post-apostolic) epistle of Peter, it is Christ the shepherd who hands over his office to men, to Peter and his 'fellow presbyters', until the time when he himself appears again as shepherd (1 Pet 5:4). Therefore, the post-apostolic ministry is marked by the consciousness of its mission from Christ and its representation of Christ.

It may be objected that, after all, each individual Christian can 'represent' Christ to another. But sacramental and official representation of Christ expresses something about the specific manner of the communication of salvation; in the official ministry the Lord does not link his salvific gift to 'the proof of the Spirit and of the power of a human being', that is, to a man's subjective charismatic endowment to be proved on each occasion, but instead to the official mission given by ordination and the gift of the Spirit, from which the believer can be sure that he is meeting Christ in the official action of the ministry. The official action with its objectivity at first seems strange, but in it Christ's effective promise of salvation is transmitted, and the action links the believer not to a human person but to the objective reality of Christ himself. This will be discussed later (p. 61ff).

At any rate, it is clear that the common priesthood of the faithful and the special official priesthood are situated on two quite different levels. The former consists of the priestly manner of life of all the baptised with Christ: the latter is 'the visible way in which the priestly mediation of Christ is made manifest.' The bearers of Church office are 'living instruments of Christ the mediator, and not delegates of the priestly people' (A. Vanhope). Thus, an essential feature of apostolic office is continued in the priestly ministry, which originates in the 'objectivity' of ordination, i.e. in an action of Christ: the Lord himself calls and empowers men in order that, through preaching and sacred signs, through pastoral instruction and service, they may equip their brothers and sisters 'for the building up of the body of Christ.'

The papal Commission for the Laity, in a document entitled 'Priests in lay associations', has given a terse and pithy summary of this point: 'As a person appointed to represent Christ for the service of this "chosen race", and as a guarantor for the maintenance of its identity, the priest has the official responsibility of seeing that the common priesthood is lived. . . . All priestly action consequently is obliged to facilitate for one and all their salvific contact with the Lord.'

2. From apostolic office to post-apostolic office

a) *Continuity in discontinuity* It is not necessary here to go into the individual historical details of the transition from apostolic to post-apostolic office, especially since there is still no consensus on the historical and exegetic features of that development. It is questionable if there was a unitary and continuous tradition, since in the New Testament there is no order and theology of ministry which can be expressed in one concept. Purely from a historical point of view, the sceptical remark of W. Pesch may well prove correct: 'There is no clear teaching in the Pauline writings, and not even in the whole New Testament, concerning priesthood and the basic elements of authority in a Christian church. There are merely occasional remarks, not always reconcilable with each other, and indeed sometimes contradictory, coming from individual theologians and in writings directed to individual local communities'. The teaching of the Church and of theologians about church office does not need any facile harmonising or smoothing out of historical questions. It is simply not possible to go along with H. Schlier's thesis that 'the continuity of the post-apostolic offices with the apostolic ministry is not merely factual and at the same time ideal, but formal and in accordance with law: it is not a mere continuity of functions but of authorisation, mandate and mission'. Although Paul certainly had already delegated his authority, it is more than questionable if this involved a delegation to a 'successor' or if the local Churches did not consider themselves empowered to appoint office-bearers. Moreover, the actual structure of ministry up to the beginning of the second century was manifold and in a state of flux. It was from this time that the so-called 'three-part ministry' (bishop, priest, deacon) became prevalent.

These first post-apostolic decades must be interpreted as a time of tentative experiment. The manifold changes of structure can be understood if one considers that the Church was then like a building under construction. The workers required for erecting a house are different from those who are needed for the administration, organisation and renovation of an already existing building. But even such an explanation can be quite inconclusive. Only one extremely surprising fact is theologically important: after a period of only a few years (in which plurality and broad variety of authority structure were dominant), the post-apostolic Church presents itself as an entity of uniform outline, which takes its continuity with the apostolic Church for granted and is accepted as such.

The speed and universality of this development and the fact that it implies unanimity in theological understanding of church office are often obscured by statements of the following kind: 'The later authority structure in the Church gradually "developed" from the New Testament beginnings'. If one remembers that the churches from Syria to Rome, without central direction (in the limited communication possibilities of the time) found the same solution within fewer than thirty years, this fact itself needs to be explained. It is not enough to offer obscure statements like 'it developed' and propose these as the ultimate explanation. Obviously, the influence of the nascent New Testament theology of church authority (as also the influence of the Spirit working in the Church) led to this surprising result.

Already in the first epistle of Clement (about 90 A.D.) the continuity and even the 'succession' of the apostolic office is reflected. 'The Apostles received the Gospel from the Lord Jesus Christ for us. Jesus the Christ was sent from God. Therefore, the Christ comes from God, and the Apostles come from Christ: both happened in good order according to God's will. . . . So they preached in city and country, and appointed their first disciples, after testing them by the Spirit, to be bishops and deacons of the future believers. . . . Our Apostles also knew . . . that there would be strife about the title of bishop. For this reason, therefore, since they had received perfect foreknowledge, they appointed the above-mentioned men, and then gave instructions that if they died, other approved men should take over their ministry'(1 Clem 42:1ff; 44:1). There is a tendency, particularly among Evangelical theologians, to interpret the first epistle of Clement as 'historical reconstruction' (P. Meinhold) of an authority which includes leadership of the community and the celebration of the Eucharist and which is clearly contrasted with the laity, here mentioned as such for the first time (40:5).But even if 'historical reconstruction' did have some influence, Clement is taking up beginnings already present in Tradition (cf. p. 49 supra). For as early as the time of the New Testament the 'building up' of the Church was going on without interruption, in a manner analogous to the laying of its apostolic foundation — that is, through minsters called and empowered by the Lord, who not merely 'represented' the apostolic foundation of the Church, but 'represented' him. In this respect, at the beginning of the second century, Ignatius of Antioch also says emphatically, 'Each one whom the Lord of the house sends to administer his house must be accepted by us as we accept the one who sends him' (Ign/Eph 6:1).

b) *The significance of the laying-on of hands and consecration* Post-apostolic Church authority was transmitted through the laying-on of hands by authorised office-bearers.

Recently E. Schillebeeckx has sought to reduce the significance of the laying-on of hands. He regards it indeed as a rite full of meaning, but he doubts whether it was and must always be the *conditio sine qua non* of appointment to the ministry. According to the *Apostolic Constitution* of Hippolytus and other documents, a 'confessor' (as a proved bearer of the Spirit) could be admitted into the presbyterium, even without the laying-on of hands. Since this has actually occurred in the past, Schillebeeckx asks, is an alternative method of appointment perhaps conceivable in the Church of today and of the future? Moreover, does not the example of the confessor admitted into the presbyterium without the laying-on of hands show that a person who has proved himself to be a charismatic, and who is accepted as such by the community, is by that very fact an office-bearer? Against this, one must say that the evidence adduced by Schillebeeckx is, from a historical point of view, far too sparse and too controverted to permit such conclusions. All the evidence derives ultimately from one passage in Hippolytus, which was immediately corrected in the Syriac version of the *Traditio Apostolica*. Moreover, it is extremely doubtful whether the confessor admitted into the presbyterium without the laying-on of hands was equal to the other presbyters in *dignity* only or could take over their *function* (e.g., celebrate the Eucharist).

C. Vogel also proposes abundant historical evidence to show that the imposition of hands was not the only rite of appointment to office. In addition, he points out that carrying out the rite of ordination did not make the ordained person an office-bearer, as it were, automatically: but that the 'ecclesial context', particularly recognition by the Church, was necessary as well. From this he draws the conclusion that the essential part of the transmission of authority was not consecration by the imposition of hands, but the recognition of a candidate as an office-bearer by the Church. This conclusion goes far beyond the historical evidence. According to the evidence, the transmission of authority was always carried out with a particular sacramental rite or in a sacramental context. Thus, what Vogel proves historically is that at first there was a variation in the sacramental signs for ordination which were recognised in the Church. If these were effective sacramental signs only when a series of juridical and ecclesiological conditions was fulfilled (e.g., true faith of the ordinand, agreement of the Metropolitan, etc.), that is no proof that recognition by the Church was the decisive factor. It merely shows that, in addition to the sacramental ordination, other conditions had to be fulfilled (cf. p. 93). Our assertion therefore stands: church office is transmitted by a sacramental sign, which principally consists of the laying on of hands — allowing for a certain amount of variety in antiquity.

Already in the later writings of the New Testament canon the imposition of hands is quite taken for granted (Acts 6:6; 1 Tim 4:14; 1 Tim 5:22; 2 Tim 1:6). It was probably taken over from the Rabbinate where it was interpreted as a 'commissioning rite' and not as a 'gesture of blessing and salvation'. This commissioning gave the power of God's spirit, and the authority to speak and act in the name of God. The Christian laying-on of hands signifies as well the link with Jesus Christ and with the apostolic origin of the Church. It is the Spirit, transmitted by this rite, who fills the one ordained and takes him over for service in the Church (cf. 2 Tim 1:6ff).

Consequently, the decree *Presbyterorum ordinis* (no. 12) rightly connected ordination (*consecratio* — a word also used in the early Church to denote baptism) with the Johannine concept of 'sanctification' (cf. Jn 10:36). To be consecrated and to be sanctified mean to be dispossessed of oneself and to be handed over to God, for a life of service and for a special mission. Moreover, the Holy Spirit is efficaciously transmitted through consecration. 'God grants to the person called by him the charisma which enables him to carry on his office' (E. Lohse) and makes him an 'instrument' of the Kyrios.

From this, two conclusions can be drawn. *First*: the alternative frequently proposed to-day, 'office or charisma', is completely untenable. Appointment to church office takes place in a rite which confers a special charisma of the Spirit. *Second*: the imposition of hands is more than a mere public authentication in and through the Church. Because the Spirit of God is conferred through this sacramental sign, it becomes immediately obvious that, from the start, installation in church office was not understood merely as 'appointment' or 'juridical transfer of power', but as a 'conferring of the Spirit.' It is, therefore, not enough to say that ordination, 'in the last analysis, is no more than an official commissioning for the service of the community' (K. H. Ohlig and H. Schüster). In ordination there is not simply a testing and certification of an already existing charisma, but the charisma is 'conferred', as H. Küng rightly says: he then continues with the question: 'Is not something essential in the ordination being overlooked, if this charisma of ministry, this special grant of the Spirit, is overlooked?' As E. Schillebeeckx rightly says, 'just as charisma without office is in danger of evaporating into sentimentality, fanaticism and mere subjectivism', in the same way office without charisma becomes stunted and 'is in danger of turning into a power-structure'.

The imposition of hands does not mean that the charisma flows as it were from the consecrator to consecrated. The charisma is rather given directly by God, a gift of the Holy Spirit himself. Consequently, the consecration is performed firstly by official ministers, who by their office show the priority of God's action; and secondly 'the Christian ordination is not performed in silence: the gift is prayed for' (G. Kretschmar). In this it becomes clear that the Holy Spirit is not only a gift to the one ordained but also to the whole praying community: in the ordination rite an effect is produced in the ordained which benefits the whole community. Jesus Christ gives himself to the ordained, for an efficacious service for the others of the faithful. The Lord 'makes himself dependent' on the person through whom he wishes to pass on his gift of salvation effectively in the future.

The imposition of hands does not only confer the Spirit and transmit ministerial authority. It also inducts the one ordained into the college of bishops or presbyters, which is formally and materially in the line of succession to the authority of the Apostles. This *successio apostolica* is not simply a mechanical chain of the imposition of hands on each individual in turn; it is also the unceasing invocation of the Holy Spirit upon candidates called by God (and, as will be seen later, agreed and accepted by the community) and their admission into the apostolic college which has the particular responsibility of representing the apostolic origin which sets the norm for the Church. Thus through the imposition of hands — that is, through consecration, conferring of the Spirit, passing on of the official mission and incorporation into the succession of the Apostles — a man is made capable of acting *in persona Christi*.

Because this profoundly spiritual event is brought about by means of the visible sign of imposition of hands — apparently so trivial and fortuitous — ordination seems a somewhat arbitrary affair. Why is an official mission given through laying-on of hands? Why not in another way? Why must it be through men who are in the *successio apostolica*? Why does the one on whom hands have been laid now have another position, another responsibility and competence in the Church?

The 'positive' character of the imposition of hands, which is laid down as an unalterable rule, 'thus and not otherwise', is, as J. Ratzinger correctly observes, in harmony with the positive nature of Christianity, its permanent essence of being something introduced from without. For this reason the imposition of hands is primarily not a symbol of the transmission of power from the community, but of the fact that in Christianity spiritual power comes, not from within and from below, but from above and from without, that is, it is a symbol for the action of the Pneuma himself, an action which is independent of the community.

c) *Church office and the commission to celebrate the Eucharist*   The fundamental duties of church office, as it appears at the beginning of the second century, include also celebration of the Eucharist. We saw already that the apostolic preaching represents the (priestly) self-sacrifice of Jesus Christ as an opportunity and a challenge, in such a way that it is the Lord himself who is present and comes to us in the words of the Apostle. Nevertheless, the word is not the only way in which he communicates himself. In Baptism and the eucharistic banquet Jesus Christ also (particularly) manifests himself sacramentally, and gives a share in his way, his truth and his life. The preached word and the celebration of the sacraments are very closely coordinated: there is no sacrament without proclamation of the word, and there is no proclamation of the word which does not — at least! — include *the* sacrament which is the listening Church itself. Therefore, just as the Kyrios promises to be present in the word of the specially appointed ministers, so also he is the real host of the eucharistic celebration, since these ministers 'represent' him in the administration of the sacraments. Consequently the presiding host-function at the celebration of the Eucharist belongs to those who are called to the special ministry of the word, and who found and lead communities in the name of this word.

Certainly it is not true that at the beginning of the Church the Eucharist was in an entirely special way the centre of the official ministry. 'It was only gradually that it became clear that the Eucharist is the most effective and the most intrinsic representation of the sacrifice of Christ, and the central requirement for the building up of the Church. As a result the priesthood was seen to be ultimately but by no means exclusively orientated to this mode of representing the priestly action of Jesus Christ. It could also be put in this way: the ministry of the priest within the Church became clarified only gradually, on the basis and model of Christ's priestly office. This in its turn consisted, not exclusively, but essentially, in his obedient submission. It was therefore necessarily understood as belonging to his prophetical and pastoral office, inseparable from his submission, and was carried out also in this office. Consequently, priestly office in the Church, which represents this offering of Christ, is one and yet manifold: it does not relate to the Eucharist alone, but it does have as its central feature this manner of making present the sacrifice of Jesus Christ' (H. Schlier). Therefore, the office-bearer in the

Church does not preside at the eucharistic celebration because he is a priest; rather, he is a priest because he presides at that celebration at which the sacrifice of Christ is made present.

The linking of the Eucharist to church office which represents Christ shows sacramentally that the community does not control the Eucharist, but that Christ himself is the one who provides the banquet, which the community receives as a gift coming to them from the Lord. Moreover, the office-bearer, who is exercising his ministry in communion with his fellow-bishops and priests is a guarantee that the community-Eucharist can be celebrated in unity with the other local churches.

The express connection of the eucharistic celebration with church office also explains why thenceforward the 'old' names 'president', 'presbyter', 'minister' were replaced by 'priest' and why the official Church regarded itself as a priestly authority. Since then, this has become the current manner of speaking; and it should not be abandoned, provided that its exact meaning and limits are clear: the priestly character of the official Church must be referred to the specific priesthood of Christ, and must not be restricted to the sacerdotal and cultic aspect.

In recent years, particularly on account of the shortage of priests, more people have been asking about whether a eucharistic celebration might not be conducted by a lay person; some, indeed, are convinced that this is quite possible and are already experimenting in this direction. Different authors defend the theory or even the practice in different ways: a) it is said that in the primitive Church a layman could preside at the eucharistic celebration; b) while still keeping to the principle enunciated by Ignatius of Antioch, 'Let only that Eucharist be held to be valid, which is celebrated under the presidency of the bishop or of the one whom he appoints', it is believed that a non-priest could then, and now, be commissioned by the bishop; c) reference is made to the concept, rooted in church history, of an 'emergency Eucharist'.

Let us examine these different arguments:

Regarding a) It is no longer possible to decide with certainty whether or not the celebration of the Eucharist was led by special officials in the time of the Apostles and in the early Church. Even the reference in the *Didache* (10, 7) — 'lay' prophets could celebrate the Eucharist

— is not decisive, since it is extremely doubtful whether these were charismatic 'laymen' (in the modern sense). Since these 'prophets' are described as 'archpriests' of the community in *Didache* 13, 3, it is much more probable that they were non-local (roving) 'apostles' who did actually possess particular and recognised authority. Both the argument from silence (i.e. we have no knowledge of an official leadership) and the opposing argument stand on weak foundations. H. Küng's assertion that 'in Corinth, the Eucharist was celebrated without a permanent community leader, responsible for the congregation', is not only based on such an *argumentum ex silentio*, but is also contrary to some historical facts. For example: the eucharistic assemblies 'took place in a patriarchically organised world, in which the presidency of the house community, and particularly of a banquet with religious character (paschal meal), did not lie in the discretion of individuals, but was carried out according to established norms' (J. Kremer). With this assertion Kremer takes up an exegetical study by B. Holmberg which shows that part of Paul's activity in organising a community was to seek out and appoint a head of household to be the host, who probably would then be the leader of the divine service.

At any rate, the celebration of the Eucharist was carried out according to apostolic directions, and in the context of an apostolic ordinance. The line of development from this arrangement to the later express commissioning of office-bearers for the celebration of the Eucharist may be long; but the difference in principle is not very great. But finally — quite independent of the force of the individual links in the chain of argument — when H. Küng proposes the global conclusion that it is 'incomprehensible why what was valid in Greece in the time of Paul should be invalid in the Italy of today,' one can equally globally remark, that there are developments in the Church which are irreversible. For example, before what is called the Council of the Apostles it was still possible to proclaim a general obligation of circumcision as an absolute prerequisite for faith in Jesus Christ: but no longer after that Council. The Church had then, through the influence of the Spirit, come to a realisation which it could not abandon without losing its identity. In the same way, the attribution of the eucharistic presidency to the ordained community leader comes from a deeper realisation of the nature of ministry and Eucharist.

Regarding b) The argument that non-priests were commissioned for the celebration of the Eucharist is unproven. That the (unordained) presbyters mentioned in *Apostolic Tradition* of Hippolytus (cf. p. 54) could also celebrate the Eucharist, is disputed: and even if they could, it was not a question of 'laymen' but of presbyters who had been received into the presbyterium in another way.

Regarding c) The suggestion that the concept of 'emergency Eucharist' is to be found in the history of the Church provides no support either. E. Schillebeeckx quotes a remark of Tertullian to this effect: but this remark comes from Tertullian's non-Catholic and Montanist period. This shows the history and intellectual background of the theory and practice of lay presidency at the Eucharist: in the history of the Church there have always been charismatic sects of enthusiasts — movements which denied the transmission of salvation through sacrament and institution or reduced it in importance, and which assigned to laymen the right to preside at the Eucharist.

Nevertheless, it cannot be absolutely ruled out that in a situation of extreme necessity, such as in a Church suffering persecution and without a priest, it could be useful to reproduce the symbols of the eucharistic celebration, even in the absence of an ordained office-bearer, in order to commemorate the Lord. (Of course one may ask if a persecuted Christian or a persecuted Christian community does not, in practice, live so closely united to the Lord in his eucharistic offering of his death, that the sacramental sign of the eucharistic celebration adds nothing to union with the Lord and with one another, and thus does not have such absolute importance.) The question whether the celebration of the 'emergency Eucharist' occupies the same sacramental position as other eucharistic celebrations may be left aside. After all, in the realm of signs there is not just a simple 'yes or no', but a fluid transition — like the transition from the so-called seven sacraments to the sacramentals, which is not sharply marked.

The situation is to be judged differently if an individual or a community disregards the directions of the Church, and without authority celebrates the Eucharist without a priest. W. Kasper says that an eucharistic celebration contrary to the authority of the Church would be 'an absurdity which would destroy the inmost essence of the Eucharist; what should be the sign of unity would become an expression of conflict'. Consequently the opinion of E. Schillebeeckx is to be rejected: he holds that practices could be developed, which would 'for a time' be in competition with officially sanctioned practices, in the hope that what was for the moment illicit would be later legitimised. In this way the sacrament of unity would become a sign of controversy, and thus robbed of all meaning.

3. The theological significance of church office as representation of Christ

Although the office of the Apostles was and still is primary, nevertheless church office, which is historically and formally in unbroken succession to it, presents fundamentally the same structure and intrinsic form. As long as it remains related to the normative apostolic witness, it re-presents the word and work of Jesus Christ himself in and for the Church. As representing Christ it is therefore also distinct from the rest of the believers and their spiritual gifts.[4]

I shall now go on to examine in more detail the meaning of church office or authority.

a) *Sacramental nature and official character of representation* The priest represents Christ, not primarily in virtue of his personal talent and skill, but in virtue of the official ministry handed over to him in his ordination. As I have pointed out earlier the word *Amt* (office, ministry) is somewhat unpopular because it easily becomes associated with the impersonality of an institution, bureaucracy, administration, organisation. The individual 'feels that he has been handed over to an overpowerful and impersonal structure'; the 'official Church' appears as an 'impersonal function', indeed as impersonal by definition; in it, it is argued, there is little sign of the personal love of its Lord and Master; like other institutions it does not escape the danger of paralysis and rigidity of routine and resistance to change, of degenerating into a bureaucratically managed structure, in which all personal life is threatened with suffocation (M. Kehl). Seen in this way the 'official' is the complete contradiction of the 'personal', above all of personal freedom.

But this is only one form of authority, and a perverted one, which does indeed exist but is foreign to the nature of church authority. Mediation through the official Church does not have to impede direct personal contact: it is to be understood as making this contact possible. The Lord does not link his salvific work to the subjective ability of particular individuals, but to a permanent, certain, definitive institutional entity which transcends the individual office-bearer, which of its nature points beyond itself to its original source and foundation — to Jesus Christ himself. He does not direct men to a deputy who takes his place (in the wrong sense); he does not leave the furtherance of his salvific work to the contingency and caprice, to the ambiguity and danger, of the varying abilities of the persons who are passing on salvation: instead, through ordination and mission he himself produces a sacrament of his presence which transcends the individual office-bearer — the official Church, through which he gives himself and his salvation. From this point of view, the official character of the transmission of salvation is something profoundly liberating for faith: its immediate contact with God is not obstructed and suppressed: neither by an attachment to the religious excellence and the subjective religious emotion of an individual nor by his limitations and wretchedness.

The believer is not directed to the personality of the office-bearer in order to meet Christ, but to his official position passed on to him by ordination, an office which is discharged in particular functions guaranteed by Christ. In this way, because of its institutional and suprapersonal character, the office is no more than a visible and sacramental instrument of immediate contact with God: it does not destroy this contact. Augustine has already pointed this out: 'If the Lord Jesus Christ had so wished, he could have granted to any one of his servants the power to administer his Baptism in his stead, giving away the power to baptise and handing it over to any one of his servants and attaching to the Baptism delegated to the servant the same power which a Baptism administered by the Lord would have had. *But this he did not wish to do* in order that the hope of the baptised might be placed in the one whom they knew to have baptised them. Therefore, he did not wish that the servant should put his hope in the servant'. The cooperation of the minister is *only* an official sign of what the Lord *himself* is doing. Consequently, church office when understood as a representation of Christ is not a search for domination, but an expression of a firm belief that Christ alone is the Lord of the Church (H.J. Pottneyer). Also there is no question in the case of priestly office of an 'objectivising' of a Church authority which initially was of charismatic origin, as M. Weber thinks, but rather the 'objectivisation' has itself a theological origin — to be an impersonal (and in this sense 'objective') sign for the Lord.

Therefore, the official Church is actually a 'sacrament of Christ'. Priestly ordination and the priestly actions which derive from it fulfil the definition of all sacraments: something perceptible to the senses (bread, wine, laying-on of hands, the words of consent in marriage or — similar signs in a living context — a common meal, the official actions of the priest, the pattern of married life) through the operation of Christ and his Spirit becomes a medium through which something far higher can be discerned: something earthly, and thus easily perceptible, something ordinary, something lowly, becomes the sign of what is highest and most important; in it Christ gives himself and his gift.

It is sometimes wonderful how in human relations ridiculously small signs can suggest something great and make it present. In his *Kleine Sakramentenlehre* Leonardo Boff describes an incident in his life. He is a South American and lived for a long time in Germany. While there, he received a letter one day giving the news of his father's death. Enclosed in the letter was the butt of the last cigarette smoked by his father. From that time on he preserved this cigarette-butt, because, as he writes: 'From that moment the cigarette-butt is no longer simply that. It became a sacrament, it lives, it tells of life, and accompanies my life.... It causes the form of our father to become present in our memory, our father who now — after the passage of some years — has become the archetype of our family and its centre of unity.' A completely valueless thing, indeed the most worthless thing possible — a cigarette-end — can become a 'sacrament', a sign that endlessly points beyond itself, to something of the utmost value, and makes it present. The difference between the sign and what it signifies is no obstacle.

Something similar but much more profound can be said about the sacramental signs of the Christian faith. The difference between the sign and what is signified is immense, and can only be overcome by faith. Augustine has said: 'Things are called sacraments since by our sight we perceive something in them, but by our intelligence we perceive in them something else. What we see has a form perceptible to the senses; what we understand contains spiritual nourishment.' Only the eyes of faith can recognise that the Lord himself is at work in the lowliness, poverty and ambiguity of the sign. The office transmitted by ordination is — considered in itself — such a sign, easily perceptible, lowly, often even pitiable, and capable of many meanings, yet a sign which points beyond itself to the salvific action of Christ and makes it present. The office-bearer also stands before the community as a sacramental sign of this kind. Because it is the priest's office that points to Christ, it is inadmissible that he should put himself in place of Christ. Just because church office is a sacramental sign which is utterly different from what is signified, it represents Christ sacramentally ...; 'it is not identical with him but is different from him in the way in which every representative/deputy differs from the one represented' (H.J. Pottmeyer).

Of course, the more decidedly the priest seeks to increase the credibility and fruitfulness of his ministry by devoting his life to the service of his cause, keeping his own personality in the background, and the more he makes Christ shine through in his own personal life, the less repellent, the more appealing and effective will his ministry be. This will be discussed later (pp. 108ff).

Since the Lord established church office to 'represent' him, and since he made effective ecclesial salvific action dependent on it (legitimated by ordination), official ministers are a visible and concrete reminder to the community of the faithful that the Church depends on Christ and is not the owner and still less the mistress of the gifts of salvation. N. Lohfink puts it very well: 'To be a priest means to bear witness to something wonderful': that is, to the amazing fact that the Church is a permanent foundation, gift and grace of God. On account of its authority structure, it is as it were inscribed in the 'blueprint' of the Church that the community of the faithful can never be self-sufficient: it has no control over the word enabling it to seek out teachers as it sees fit (cf. 2 Tim 4:3f); it has no control over the sacraments enabling it to celebrate them simply at will; it has no control over church order, enabling it to brush order aside in a moment of enthusiasm. In the contrast between the official creed and any individual private belief we see the basic *differentia* which constitutes the Church: the Church is *ek-klesia*, called together by *God*; its foundation is outside itself — in Jesus Christ.[5]

b) *Unity of testimony and witness* The theological significance of church office is still to be clarified from another point of view. Because the Church is the *creatura verbi*, it has before it the word of God; Scripture gives it a promise of salvation and of holiness and constitutes a standard by which it is to be judged. But Scripture is not a 'hypotasised' word; that is, it is not an independent entity; as Scripture points out, it itself is dependent on the appointed witness[6] who is an obedient hearer of the word and is sent to give testimony. There is therefore a reciprocal relation between the word of God which operates through personal testimony, and the office of witness which is constituted by listening to the word and by being sent by the word. In all this, the witness is testifying to something which precedes him and which is outside his control; on the other hand, the word to which he testifies is dependent on him for the place and manner of its expression: through him it acquires communicable form. Thus word and witness form an indissoluble unity. They are what they are by sharing in this giving of testimony, each by a contribution of self — the original antecedent word giving testimony of itself, and the witness living from and in his experience of the antecedent word (E. Kienzler).

This inseparable unity of word and witness reaches its culmination in Jesus Christ himself. He 'is his own cause in person': i.e., with him there is a perfect unity of *what* is proclaimed and *who* proclaims it. This unity which reaches its height in him was already manifested before him in the mission of the prophets and after him is manifested in the official Church. As W. Kasper remarks, it is part of 'the fundamental structure of the Church that the cause of the Gospel is linked to witnesses of the Gospel who are sent with full authority.' This is also clearly stated in Scripture. Our exposition of 2 Cor 5:18f has already shown that the ministry of reconciliation was founded simultaneously with the 'fact' of the reconciliation (a similar interlocking of the two is to be found in Rom 10:14f and often). For this reason an ecumenical study* says that 'Paul spoke of the Gospel as being his Gospel, in such a way that the Apostle and his Gospel cannot be separated from one another. Certainly not only the *content* of the apostolic testimony but also the act of witnessing to the apostolic message are of authoritative importance. To accept the Apostles does not mean merely to repeat their words: it means to continue their work and to promote the proclamation of God's salvific action to the world.' But if this 'continuation' of the action of the Apostles does not simply mean the repetition of the content of their words, but also of the style of their action, the word of God must continue to be proclaimed in strict connection with authorised witnesses. Consequently, the permanent apostolicity of the Church must include not only the *content* of its preaching and its faith, but as well the *manner* in which this content is transmitted, namely through authoritative testimony. And this is what church office does.

If the reciprocal interrelation between the witness and his testimony is destroyed, two (opposing) dangers arise.

1. If the word is independent of legitimate witnesses, it necessarily becomes an uncontrollable 'word happening', which comes about wherever and whenever it will. This means that it not only becomes intangible but also ultimately subject to 'manipulation' by the person or persons who claim to be the location of this 'happening' (this is the danger for Protestants).

2. Where, on the contrary, the official Church is no longer strictly bound to the word, it loses the proper justification for its existence, its essential relation to God's word, and then it binds the hearer to its own human authority (this is the danger for Catholics).

It is only in the indissoluble relationship of testimony and authorised witness, a relationship which persists in church office and which is established by ordination, that the Church continues to be under the word of God as the *creatura verbi*.

c) *The concrete handing on of God's pastoral care*   The theological position of a special priestly office within the people of God is also clear from another point of view. H. Schürmann says that 'the centre and climax of all the New Testament statements about the office of the one who presides' is the duty of the shepherd. The original and proper application of the shepherd metaphor is the all-embracing care of God for Israel. But even in the Old Testament, God, the true and proper 'shepherd' of men, sent shepherds in whom his pastoral care took concrete form and became perceptible to men. Finally, it is Jesus who in his utterly selfless devotion to the flock shows in action what God's shepherding of his people means. The shepherd-office of Jesus, which claimed his whole life, is continued in the apostolic (Jn 21:15-19) and post-apostolic (Eph 4:11) ministry. The metaphor of the shepherd makes clear that 'between shepherd and flock there is an essential distinction which excludes all identification but which signifies a reciprocal relationship. ... Opposition and reciprocity are the essential features of the shepherd-flock metaphor' (H. Urs v. Balthasar). This has absolutely nothing to do with a claim of the shepherd to any superiority over the flock or with a hierarchical system of caste which makes false claims to a freedom-destroying authority (no matter how loudly the 'war cries' may be which are ringing out today). Already in the Old Testament the life of the shepherds appointed by God was 'a series of hardships: they are utilised to the full, their mistakes are strictly punished. ... They experience persecution, rebellion, betrayal ..., they become more and more "sufferers for the people"' (H. Urs v. Balthasar).

In quite the same way, Christ is the 'shepherd struck down' (Mk 14:27). In following him Peter receives together with the office of shepherd the promise that he himself will be totally dispossessed of himself and will be led to the cross. Similarly Paul, defending his authority, has to say about himself: 'afflicted in every way, but not crushed; perplexed but not despairing; persecuted but not abandoned; struck down but not destroyed; wherever we go, we always carry the death of Jesus in our body, so that the life of Jesus also may be manifested in our body. For we who live are being constantly delivered up to death for the sake of Christ, that the life of Jesus also may be manifested in our mortal flesh' (2 Cor 4:8ff). It is precisely because he is the shepherd 'delivered up to death' that he is able to demand that the community obey and follow him.

The same is true of the post-apostolic ministry, as can be gathered from the first epistle of Peter. In it the writer, as a 'witness of the sufferings of Christ' warns his 'fellow presbyters' to care for the flock entrusted to them, and to be a pattern for it (*forma gregis*: 1 Pet 5:11ff), a term which E. Schillebeeckx paraphrases as 'essential image of the community.' This warning occurs in a context which identifies pastoral care with suffering — suffering for and with the flock.

In all these texts there is no trace of any hierarchical triumphalism or of holiness pertaining to an élite. They indicate, on the contrary, a special ministry of leadership and devotion to the flock which does not derive from the community or from other 'charismatic' vocations. This ministry is not divisible into separate single functions, just as the duty of the shepherd is indivisible. Neither is it a matter — at least primarily — of the functions of organisation and administration which every social group requires: it involves instead toil and suffering — leading even to crucifixion — in order that Christ may be formed in the flock which has been entrusted to the minister, as Paul says: 'my children, once more am I in travail with you until Christ be formed in you' (Gal 4:19). This means equipping the baptised 'to fulfil their service, for the building up of the body of Christ' (Eph 4:12), and gathering together the whole of humanity into the people of God, to join with Christ in offering to the Father the sacrifice of all creation.

The role of the shepherd expresses — and rightly — his difference from the flock. Nevertheless, it must not be overlooked that the shepherd also with *at least* equal necessity has his place entirely inside the flock. For *firstly*, like every Christian, and together with everyone else, he also needs to be rescued by the grace of Christ, the 'chief Shepherd'; *secondly*, both shepherd and flock, in spite of their diversity of function, are absolutely dependent on one another and yoked together into the unity of the people of God, in a multiple and reciprocal spiritual interchange of giving and receiving (cf. p. 42); and *thirdly* the shepherd causes his fellow-Christians to share in his responsibility. As a particular pastoral service to the many other charismata, the office-bearer must awaken spiritual talents, discover them and stimulate their possessors to take on tasks in the Church and the world. Thus it belongs to the office of shepherd in the Church to be surrounded *by many fellow-workers and helpers*. Paul had already expected these others also to be accepted by the community, without for that reason becoming pastors responsible for it.

This must be the starting-point of the discussion about the new part-time and full-time pastoral ministries. Where *pastoral* ministries of *lay* cooperators and assistants are concerned (note: it is not a question of purely lay ministries, but of the pastoral activity of lay cooperators), the ministries remain 'orientated to the ordained pastors and dependent on them' (H. Socha). But if laymen are *de facto* more or less independent pastors in a community and are commissioned to preach the word of

God, if they are acknowledged as such by the community and are sent by the bishop to fill a vacant place because no priest is available, these should be *ordained*. Otherwise the impression is given that the sacrament of holy orders and the power conferred by it are not in fact all that necessary for pastoral ministry in the Church. At any rate 'only those persons can have authority in the Church who have received the pastoral sacrament of ordination. This is a fundamental structural principle of the Church, and it is violated if pastoral assistants assume powers of leadership in virtue of a legal act alone, if they represent the Church — especially as persons to whom people apply in vacant parishes — without being empowered to represent Christ for it. . . . In this situation the question must not be asked: Is it, then, possible to dispense with ordination? On the contrary. The holders of diaconal and priestly office must be equipped by the sacrament of holy orders, so that the dependence on God's mercy may become unambiguously visible' (H. Socha). If Church law on celibacy proved to be a hindrance to ordination, the conditions for admission would need to be changed — subject to all the qualifications and limitations yet to be discussed (cf. pp. 120ff). For ecclesiastical regulations — no matter how sensible they be — ought not interfere with and destroy the sacramental structure of ministry and Church.

We have examined the theological import of post-apostolic office from a number of different angles. We have seen that it is a ministry with the same basic structure as apostolic ministry. The priest also is a 'steward of the mysteries of God' (1 Cor 4:1), and that means that his duty is to serve as a cooperator in the salvific action of God in Jesus Christ (which Paul calls '*mysterion*').

The special cooperation of the ministry is depicted in the New Testament image of the 'fishers of men' (Mk 1:17; Lk 5:4ff; and also Jn 21:3ff).

At the command of the Lord and in his name the chosen disciples cast out their nets to win over men by word and deed: in the casting out of the nets by the disciples, Jesus Christ is at work: *he himself wishes to cast out by means of them the all-embracing net of his love.*

4. Summary. According to the Second Vatican Council there is an 'essential difference' between priest and layman. What does this mean?

If we consider church office under the aspect of its being representation of Christ, then it is, *within the people of God*, an essential *sacrament* of Christ, i.e., a sign and instrument of his action which it makes present. (However, there are other aspects, which we will discuss in the next chapter.)

By this we also mean that church office is not simply a collection of individual tasks or indeed of merely sacramental powers. Nowadays people often ask: What 'can' the layman do, What is it that only the priest 'can do', What power can the official Church relinquish, What could the layman also do? However, if one takes up this line of questioning, the ministry will be denuded like a rose gradually being stripped of its petals in an attempt to discover what a rose is, until in the end perhaps two petals remain — namely, the power to celebrate the Eucharist and to administer sacramental absolution. Just as what remains after the petals have been removed is no longer a rose, so, too, what is left of the ministry in the context of these questions is no longer the ministry but a caricature of it. Neither can Christ's person, mission and salvific action be broken up into individual elements or powers. It is a complete whole. In this complete whole, theological tradition, as we have seen, has emphasised three inseparable and inadequately distinct structural elements — Christ as prophet, priest and pastor, but in an indissoluble unity. Consequently, the office-bearer who is acting as Christ's representative also has the triple task: he must proclaim the word, he must be a priest and he must be a pastor. All three are inseparably part of church office. They broaden out the narrow image of the cultic priest (which was not always absent in the past) and show that his ministry is not limited to separate sacral powers and functions, but is something whole and complete in which the whole Christ is seen and is present.

As a 'sacrament of Christ' founded and authorised by ordination, the priest is not simply an 'organ' of the community, even if (as will be seen later) he is designated with the consent and sometimes even by the vote of the community. Instead — as the agreed report of the (ecumenical) Dombes Group says — he is also a 'man with a mission' whom the community receives from Christ. His functions show the priority of God's initiative and authority in the life of the Church, the continuity of the mission to the world, the common bond which the Spirit forms between the different local communities in the unity of the Church. Pope John Paul II wrote similarly in his letter for Holy Thursday 1979: 'The priest is a gift for the community, a gift which comes from Christ himself, from the fulness of his priesthood' (no. 4). This eschatological and sacramental view of official church ministry in no way destroys the fraternal unity of the people of God, nor does it take away their fundamental equality: it merely reveals the internal structure of the Church. Jesus Christ himself did not 'destroy' or 'break up' the *communio* of his disciples. Instead he was among them, holding them together as the 'head' (that is, as a special but intrinsic essential factor). In a similar way the special priestly mission does not involve separation from the community of the baptised, but leads more deeply into the life of the Church.

The ministry with authority from Christ, and the community of the other baptised, filled with the Holy Spirit and endowed with his gifts, live out 'in their mutual relationship . . . their dependence on the one Lord and High Priest' (Dombes Group).

For just as the community is dependent on the intermediary office of the official ministry, so too the office-bearer — as will be seen later — as one in need and one who receives, is dependent upon his fellow-Christians, in whom the Holy Spirit is at work. Consequently, church office and the common priesthood of the baptised are 'not properly to be regarded as superior or inferior, greater or lesser, primary and secondary, but as original and valuable aspects of their interrelation and mutual dependence'(J.W. Mödlhammer).

In this connection the Second Vatican Council has made use of the expression — easily and often misunderstood — of the 'essential difference' between the official priesthood and the universal priesthood. As the Council says both forms of priestly service differ *'essentia et non gradu tantum'* (*Lumen gentium*, no. 10); that is, the basis of their difference is not a matter simply of degree, i.e. higher or lower position: it is not merely that the official priesthood has greater 'rights' and 'powers'; it is not simply 'greater', and the common priesthood of the baptised is not 'less'. The difference between the two is *'essentia'*, of an essential kind, that is, they are indeed allied to one another, but on a completely different level which is not adequately described by the concept of domination or subordination, of 'more' or 'less'. The difference between official and lay priesthood is not primarily one of jurisdiction; it is sacramental, that is, it lies as we have seen, on the level of significant and effective *symbol*. In his distinctive relation to the rest of the community the priest is an effective sign that Christ is the Lord of the Church and is present in it with his saving work.

5. *A note on the intrinsic unity of priestly ministry*

In the last twenty-five years the question has often been asked if the threefold nature of the mission of Christ (as teacher, priest and shepherd) and correspondingly of the priest are three aspects of something higher still, or if any of the three inseparable elements includes the other two and consequently causes the unity of all three. In current theological writing this question is answered in different ways.

a) *The ministry of the word as the basis of this unity*   In the documents of the Second Vatican Council the 'proclamation of the word' is twice described as the first duty of the priestly office (*Lumen gentium*, no. 28; *Presbyterorum ordinis*, no. 4). Also, the Council debates show that some Council Fathers wished the 'service of the word' to be regarded as the all-inclusive centre of priestly activity. For this reason, J. Ratzinger believes that, according to the Council, 'the word, understood in its full depth, is the comprehensive and fundamental source from which the other two forms of official action are derived. They are the two ways in which its performance is articulated, while at the same time it always includes them'. K. Rahner was of a similar view; for him the Church collectively is *the* 'sacrament', that is, a sign and testimony of the eschatologically victorious salvific word of God in Jesus Christ. This word issues on different levels and in manifold concrete forms, and reaches its climax in three proclamations of the death and Resurrection of Christ in the celebration of the Eucharist. The priest, appointed to the ministry of the word, is consequently and in this respect also ordained for the ministry of the word, which culminates in the sacramental action and for the service of the community which is to be gathered together to hear the word and is to be led by it.

b) *Pastoral office as the basis of unity* According to the New Testament, Christ himself regarded 'the gathering up of the scattered children of God' (Jn 11:52) as his mission; as the Good Shepherd, he wishes to gather those who do not yet belong to his flock (cf. Jn 10); this is, so to speak, his last will and testament (Jn 17), that all be one. Consequently, the Church presents itself from the beginning as the *one* body of Christ, which is the sign and instrument of the unity established by the Lord (cf. e.g., 1 Cor 12; Gal 3;28; Eph 1:14ff etc.). This unity is an ongoing, permanent, responsibility, not only because it is forever endangered by sin and selfishness, but also because all the various charismata, powers and ministries produced by the Spirit need to be channelled towards mutual help. To achieve this an authority is needed whose central content is the 'ministry of maintaining unity and peace in the Church'. W. Kasper particularly has proposed this as the central function of priestly ministry. 'It must coordinate the different charismata, bring them to cooperate; it must discover charismata, give them scope, encourage them but also call them to order when they brusquely endanger and disturb the unity of the Church'.

Since the unity of the Church is a unity subject to and produced by the word, pastoral office includes the proclamation of the word; and since unity is most clearly brought about in the celebration of the sacraments, the presidency at the celebration belongs to the pastors. H. U. v. Balthasar also emphasises the pastoral task of the official Church in his more recent writings about church authority (cf. pp. 60ff).

c) *Sacerdotal action as the basis of unity* It was principally H. Schlier who took the mission of Jesus Christ, and consequently of the official Church, to be fundamentally 'priestly' in character (cf. p. 42ff). According to him the church ministry of proclaiming the word and the pastoral ministry have as their objective the representation of the radical surrender of Jesus to the Father on our behalf, even unto death. This 'new' priesthood of Christ is depicted sacramentally in all official spheres of action, but most of all in the celebration of the Eucharist.

d) *Specific mission as the basis of unity* J. Ratzinger holds to the primacy of the proclamation of the word, but sees the actual integration-point of the priestly office in a dimension which is the basis of all three central activities of the official Church — namely in the special mission received through Jesus Christ, or more precisely, in an incorporation into the mission of Christ. Looked at in this way, priesthood essentially signifies 'vicariousness', 'representation'; it always occupies only the second place to the Lord, whose will is to come himself in priestly service to mankind. This 'task of being an emissary of Jesus does not merely require a man to perform some definite activity; it affects his essence. If the nature of priesthood consists in having a mission, then this means that being-for-another is part of his essence. In a double sense one who receives a mission belongs no longer to himself: he is dispossessed of himself for the benefit of the one he represents and for the benefit of those before whom he represents him. Thus, to have a mission means having an existential tension in two directions. It means giving way entirely to the sender, the one who gives the commission; the herald and messenger does not bring himself: instead, he leaves himself out of consideration; he does not proclaim himself, does not falsify the word entrusted to him; he does not block the way to the one who sent him, or obscure him; he is ready to decrease in order that the other may increase. To learn this lesson, rigorous practice is required, which produces a change in the whole man, especially as it involves readiness at the same time to be always at the disposal of the others, to whom he is sent'. This double 'selflessness' of the office-bearer — extending vertically and horizontally — to which particularly Christ invites him, and which is made possible by ordination, constitutes the 'essence' of priestly ministry.

This integration of the triple nature of the one ministry under the aspect of mission does not prevent one from attaching different degrees of importance to the different spheres of action in the way the first three theories do (and as Ratzinger himself also does when assigning priority to the proclamation of the word).

e) *All these theories taken as one*   Which of these four explanations is supported by the best arguments?

The original question may well have been put incorrectly. If one assumes that the three spheres of activity of church office form a unity and cannot be separated or adequately distinguished from one another, then the differences in the theories is rather due to difference of approach and emphasis. They do not contain 'absolute' truth, but depend essentially on the personal vocation and ability of the individual priest, his particular field of activity and the circumstances of the time in each case. Consequently, the individual priest has a basic spiritual need, while listening to his own personal vocation and reflecting together with his brothers, to ask himself where is or where ought to be his own special task, its centre of gravity and 'style'. This approach will lead to a legitimate multiplicity of 'images of the priest' which become distorted only when the triple nature of priestly office is obscured in favour of one or two isolated elements. P. J. Cordes rightly says that 'the minister of religion who is banished to the region of cultic ministry, the community leader who must restrict himself to the management and coordination of parish departmental officials, the "prophet" who only "stimulates" but does not remain to accompany the development and whose word is not "crystallised" in the sacramental sign — all these are but impoverished forms of the one ministry. In spite of the urgent need for specialisation, such a reduction of church office to one of the three official functions seems highly questionable on theological grounds, and today it is already possible to see in "Mass-priests", "roving preachers", or "clerical administrators", the problematical pastoral consequences of such division'.

These words of P. J. Cordes, who is today an episcopal member of the Roman Curia, are unusually apposite. Do they not also cause one to think of many other impoverished forms of spiritual ministry? What about a professor of theology, who is not the leader of a local community or connected with it as a priest? What about a Roman curial official, who at a certain level must be consecrated as a bishop, although his work is purely administrative? What about a manager of church property who is solely engaged in administration alone? Important though ecclesiastical leadership and special tasks may be, the priest or bishop appointed to these responsibilities is and remains bound by the *whole* official mission: priestly office is and remains an integrated whole, which of itself must point to the whole Christ. How, therefore, can ordination have its full meaning, when a person has neither the will nor the ability nor the opportunity to realise the totality of the office, and when perhaps his only objective is a position in the Church which is institutionally secure and prominent? The celebration of Mass without a congregation is no guarantee of the full meaning of priestly ordination and priestly office.

3

Ministry and 'representation' of the Church — the ecclesial-pneumatological foundation of church office

Up to now we have been considering the priesthood chiefly in relation to Christ. The holder of church office acts sacramentally as a 'representative of Christ'; more precisely: Christ acts in and on the Church, and in doing this he also avails of special office-bearers as his co-workers. This view has been predominant in the Western Church since the Middle Ages, but it is, in the truest sense, one-sided. Church office belongs not only to Jesus Christ: it also belongs to the Church; the priest is not only an instrument of the risen Lord but also an organ of the community: because the word which he proclaims is the faith of the Church and he has a 'mission from the Church to proclaim the Gospel in its name' (K. Rahner), so much so that nothing may be preached in the Church which is not rooted in the faith and practice of the Church. The sacraments which the priest celebrates are not only sacraments of Christ but also celebrations of the community which are only valid if the office-bearer has the intention 'of doing what the *Church* does'. And up to the high Middle Ages it was taken for granted that the entire priestly Church offers the eucharistic sacrifice through the priest — not that the priest alone celebrates the Eucharist for the community in virtue of a commission from Christ. Briefly: it is in accordance with the oldest tradition of the Church that the priest is acting not only *in persona Christi* but also *in persona ecclesiae*. The ministry is not only a sacramental representation of Christ, but also a sacramental representation of the Church.

To restore the correct balance, our reflections, which up to this have been preponderantly christological, must now take a completely new direction. This will involve consideration of questions which belong to the history of theology and will throw light on a theological aspect of the question which has often been overlooked in the Western Church since the end of the Middle Ages, but which is of the utmost importance for a balanced doctrine of ministry. (Readers who are short of time and are not interested in details of the history of theology can omit pages 78-84 without losing the thread of the argument.)

1. *Exegetical and historical introduction*

a) *The concept of representation in the early Church* The idea of 'corporate personality' was familiar to the whole of ancient civilisation. It meant that 'an entire group, its dead members as well as the living and those yet to be born, can act as a single unitary entity. This the group can do through any of its members who is called to represent it' (H. Wheeler Robinson). The whole group is fully contained in this individual, usually the father or leader of the community. Thus, an entire social entity becomes concrete symbolically — visibly and effectively — in this one individual who is consequently both its representative and its leader. This does not mean that, through a legal procedure such as an election, the community delegates its full authority of action to one person, in the way in which a head of government is appointed according to modern political theory. Nor does it mean that a single individual, by consent of the others, becomes a representative 'symbol' (subject to replacement) of the community in question, somewhat as when a person becomes a ceremonial presidential head of state. In each of these cases the community is represented *by* an individual. The ancient concept of corporate personality was that a particular society is represented *in* an individual since he is the visible concrete expression of the common will, action and suffering in the organic common life of the community.

In modern society it is difficult to find anything comparable to this earlier notion of corporate personality. Since the beginning of modern times, representation is understood almost exclusively in the juridical sense of a transference of power. It is only in the less institutionalised groups (such as the family, groups of friends, etc.) that something analogous is to be found. The family, for example, 'feels' itself represented in a father (or mother); or a group of friends or a lobby will gather around one member who is as it were the 'symbolic figure' of this united group. Here we can still see something which was an essential part of the ancient idea of corporate personality: the whole life, fate and goal of a community literally grow together — 'become concrete' — in one person. This process can take place in many ways, not only through sharing and suffering of the same fate, but through a particular creative aspiration to a common goal and common tradition, through a special feeling for the circumstances and purpose of the group, as well as through the expression of its common will (this implies the seeking of counsel and assent as well as the effort to bring about a consensus). Because of such living organic relationships the 'representing' corporate personality and the particular community can become strictly interchangeable entities.

We shall later examine the notion of corporate personality in greater theological depth. At any rate it is already clear from this concept, current as it was in antiquity, that in the New Testament it was taken for granted that the office-bearer represented not merely Christ, but also the Church.

Thus, for example, the group of the twelve disciples of Jesus is not only the remote origin of the apostolate (cf. pp. 31f); it is also the nucleus of the people of God which is to be gathered anew and which they will represent. In other words, the whole future people is already represented for Jesus by 'individuals' — in fact by those individuals who would later become apostles. This situation was further developed after the Resurrection. The 'we' of the apostolic preaching (e.g. Acts 2:32) expresses not only the confession of faith of the apostolic college, but also the faith of the Church. This becomes again particularly clear in Paul. He was absolutely certain that he had received directly from the Lord a calling to be an apostle of Jesus Christ, and that he had not taken over or learned what he was preaching from a man, but had received it through the revelation of Jesus Christ. Yet, he went 'up to Jerusalem' to submit his Gospel there 'lest he be running in vain' (Gal 2:1), that is, so that he might be proclaiming *that* Gospel which was being proclaimed in the entire Church.

The apostolic office of Paul is therefore to be regarded from two points of view. 'He is an apostle, because the risen Lord has

called him and sent him: but he is an apostle only while he gives
testimony to the Gospel, in common with the other apostles' (J.
Roloff), in fact in common with the whole Church. Consequently,
if the apostle speaks and acts, the whole Church or community
speaks and acts in him. Even when he is using his authority, he
sets himself within the community. His 'children' are always at
the same time his 'brethren' also. He 'constantly invents new
compound words using the prefix *syn* (together) to emphasise his
sharing with his community in action, struggle, prayer, consolation,
suffering, rejoicing and triumph. Where he has to reprove, he
usually unites himself with his hearers with a "we" which is more
than a literary plural' (V. Campenhausen). He is convinced that
what he has to proclaim as the word of the Lord is at the same
time in accord with what the community recognises and carries
out in its profoundest Spirit-inspired reality (cf. 1 Cor 10:15; 14:37
and passim). Thus 'when Paul comes for the first time into a new
city of Asia Minor or Greece he represents not only God or Jesus
Christ, but also the Christian Church' (B. Holmberg).

If we glance at the earliest post-New Testament writings, we
see that they are frequently letters from office-bearers/communities
addressed to office-bearers/communities, without making any
distinction. Jerome expresses this later in the following words which
are difficult to translate: 'Clement wrote *ex persona Romanae
ecclesiae* (representing in his person the Roman church) to the
church of the Corinthians'. Similarly Cyprian writes, 'The bishop
is in the Church and the Church is in the bishop'. This does not
mean that the bishop is simply a constitutive part of the Church,
but that he represents it as a corporate personality, and that at
the same time the Church is conscious that it is represented in
the bishop. For this reason it is often noticeable in early
ecclesiastical texts that, in central church activities such as the
Eucharist and Penance, the office-bearer and the Church not only
join in the action but on occasion merge into one another: where
the bishop alone is mentioned, the community is frequently also
meant: where only the Church is mentioned, a specific mention
of the office-bearer is implied.

To sum up: in the accepted life of the Church, the office-bearers
were regarded not only as 'representatives' of Christ, but also as
'representatives' of their communities.

b) *Medieval views on 'twofold' representation*

It was in the eleventh and twelfth centuries that the 'twofold position' of the priest, that is, the interpretation of his two functions of acting 'in the name of Christ' and 'in the name of the Church' was for the first time expressly considered. This happened in connection with a rather surprising question: What about a priest who through heresy, excommunication or penal laicisation has lost his office? It must be emphasised that it is not a question of an 'unworthy' priest, but of one whose link with the Church is completely broken. The problem may appear to be special and unusual: but it must be remembered that the situation in the Church at that time was affected to an unusual extent by the investiture controversy and simony, by schism and heresy. Consequently, the question was a real and pressing one: Can a priest who is separated from the Church — a simoniacally ordained priest was considered to be in schism — continue to celebrate the Eucharist and in this way perform what is the integrating centre and culmination of his priestly office. The answer given by Peter Lombard and a series of theologians before and after him was a definite 'No'. Their reason was that at the consecration — held by medieval theology to be the central point of the Eucharist — 'no one says "*offero*" (I offer) but "*offerimus*" (we offer): that is, the priest speaks as it were in the name of the Church (*ex persona ecclesiae*)' (PL 192, 865). Therefore, a priest who is separated from the unity of the Church, or from whom the Church has taken away priestly authority, cannot celebrate this sacrament. He lacks the power to act 'in the name of the Church.'

Before we see that this answer of Peter Lombard is inadequate, it is useful to look at the exact meaning and the background of the expression 'in the name of the Church' (*in [ex] persona ecclesiae*). We find it used also at that time for solving two other problems. *The first problem:* How can someone who is not ready or able to forgive another nevertheless pray the petition of the Our Father 'as we also forgive those who trespass against us'? *The second problem:* How can someone who has no more than an imperfect faith (*fides informis* = faith without charity) nevertheless pray the Creed?

Both problems point to a contradiction between the interior act and its outward expression. This contradiction is resolved when one considers that the believer in question who lacks the right interior dispositions can perform his prayer or act of faith if he performs them *in persona ecclesiae*, because in the Our Father and the Creed the prayer and faith of the whole Church are expressed: it is, strictly speaking, the Church which utters this prayer and this act of faith. If, therefore, a single individual is praying, he shares in the prayer and faith of the whole Church — even if he can pray only imperfectly. He unites his personal action — very defective perhaps — with the performance of the whole Church and inserts his prayer as it were into the prayer of the Church. Thus, the formula *in* [*ex*] *persona ecclesiae* expresses the fact that there are acts of faith which are properly acts of the *communio*, of the Church, and which are significant for the individual only when he is joined to the unity of the Church.

That is the background of Peter Lombard's assertion that the celebration of the Eucharist by a priest separated from the Church was null and void. Such a priest could not use those words of the faith ('*offerimus*'), which belong primarily to the *persona ecclesiae*. It is only when he can act *in persona ecclesiae* that his priestly ministry has meaning.

Peter Lombard's commentary on the Sentences was *the* standard textbook of the Middle Ages. Such was his authority that this solution was vigorously supported. But Albert the Great and other theologians opposed it, and Thomas Aquinas used the following arguments against it: In celebrating the Eucharist the priest first of all acts and speaks *in persona Christi*; he has become Christ's instrument in virtue of his ordination. Now, since this competence cannot be lost, the sacrament, the representation of Jesus' self-offering for us on the cross, is effected. To this extent Peter Lombard is wrong when he declares that the Mass celebrated by a priest separated from the Church is totally invalid. But this is only one side of the question. At the celebration of the Eucharist not only is something done by Christ, but something is also done by the Church — its joint offering with Christ. This, however, cannot be performed sacramentally by a priest who has fallen away from the unity of the Church. To this extent the sacrament is invalid.

We see, then, that for Thomas the Eucharist — and all other basic activities of the Church as well — are characterised by a double element: 'In the Mass, when the priest "prays", he speaks in fact *in persona ecclesiae* with which he is joined in unity. At the consecration, however, he speaks *in persona Christi*, whom he represents in virtue of his ordination'. 'When he prays': these words do not refer to just any prayers during the Mass; they refer to the prayer which Peter Lombard sums up with the word *offerimus* (we offer) — a prayer which the priest utters in the name of the Church. At the Eucharist (and analogously in other salvific rites), the priest is acting in a twofold manner:

Firstly, it is Christ himself who is consecrating through the priest, i.e. he comes to us to sanctify us, raises us to community with himself, makes us capable of joining with him in his offering of himself to the Father. In this the priest is acting sacramentally and symbolically 'in the name of Christ'. *Secondly*, through him the Church speaks the *offerimus*, i.e., in the sacramental celebration it makes its offering through Christ and with him to the Father: in this the priest is acting 'in the name of the Church'.

This twofold activity of the priest is founded on the twofold movement which characterises the whole process of salvation: in Christ, God comes to mankind for the work of reconciliation and sanctification (the 'katabatic' = downward, movement), and then mankind receives from God the power to go with Christ to the Father along the way of sacrifice (the 'anabatic' = upward, movement). The unity of this twofold movement derives from the person of Christ, who as a mediator between God and man comes to us from the Father and also goes along the road with us to the Father. Therefore, in the great actions of the process of salvation, in word, sacrament and preparation for the communal ecclesial following of Christ, there is always a duality: the word, *and* the response of faith; sanctifying action *and* an answering self-surrender; guidance *and* obedient acceptance and conformity. In other words: the word of Christ becomes the answering word of belief of the Church; his salvific action becomes the principle of life in the sanctified people of God; his life becomes the form and imprint of the life of the Church community. In all this there is not a mere juxtaposition of two aspects, but an essential bipolar unity. This unity derives from the fact that the reality of Christian salvation is not solely an action of God upon men: it is also an interior drawing of men into the movement of Christ to God. From this comes the twofold 'face' of the Church: it is on the one hand the *sponsa Christi* i.e., the bride who, in her poverty and need and 'difference' from her bridegroom, receives everything as a gift from him; and on the other hand, it is the 'body of Christ', and consequently 'the fulness of him who fills all in all' (Eph 1:23). Thus, one can and must understand the Church now as distinct from Christ who comes to redeem and save it, and now as a *communio* with Christ, indeed as the *Christus totus*, that is, as a unity of head and members, a unity in which all are joined with the Lord and 'subjected to the one who subjected all things to him, that God may be all in all' (1 Cor 15:28).

The twofold viewpoint from which church office is to be regarded corresponds exactly to this dual unity of aspects. *In persona Christi* the priest is a messenger in place of Christ: as one distinct from the community he is the expression of that difference, the Church receiving from the Lord all that it possesses. But at the same time he is also a *minister ecclesiae*, an organ of the believing, praying and offering Church. As such he acts *in persona ecclesiae* when he proclaims the faith of the Church, celebrates its sacraments and works for the formation of Christ in the Church. Ordination consequently not only means a mission and authority received from Christ to act in his place: it also means authority and power to act *in persona ecclesiae* as a permanent 'servant of the Church'. This power is also sacramental and symbolic. That is: the priest is acting not in place of the Church as if he were someone delegated by it — we are not in the juridical sphere! — but as that organ through which and in which the Church is present and acting.[7] Consequently, even one who meets a priest unworthy and imperfect (in the proclamation of the word, the celebration of the sacraments, in the leading of a community) can meet the whole Church which presents itself in him.

So we come back again to the problem discussed by Peter Lombard: Can a priest separated from the Church celebrate the Eucharist? Peter Lombard answered this question with a blunt negative. Thomas Aquinas makes a more precise distinction: if the office-bearer is no longer tolerated by the Church (e.g., if he is excommunicated or deposed), he is no longer able to act *in persona ecclesiae*. Nevertheless, when he celebrates a sacrament, for example the Eucharist, the sacrament is valid — that is, the effective sign of God's salvific action is made present since the priest, in virtue of his ordination, has the irrevocable power of acting *in persona Christi*. But, on the other hand, a sacrament is not complete when God's offering of salvation is validly produced (for example, valid consecration in the Eucharist). God's saving action has a further objective — the unity of the mystical body of Christ: men are to achieve unity among themselves and go with Christ along the way to God. But this *res sacramenti*, i.e., the proper objective of the sacrament (and of all salvific actions), Thomas also teaches, is not achieved through a priest who can no longer act 'in the name of the Church'. His action is not an effective 'anabatic' response, since the Church no longer stands behind him. It is only as an *organ of the Church* that the priest can be an instrument and minister of the 'upward' movement of the Church with Christ to the Father.

This theological concept of high Scholasticism must now be explored more fully. Later it came to be expressed in juridical terms — that is, the description and reality of the action *in persona ecclesiae* were no longer understood under the aspect of organic and sacramental representation, but were regarded instead as a grant of jurisdiction by the Church. Simultaneously the sacramental action was to an extent widely treated as a material thing: it was no longer seen as the meeting-point of two personal movements — from God to man and from man to God — but instead as a legally authorised act transmitting an impersonal grace. The newer Catholic ecclesiology (which can be regarded as officially beginning with the Encyclicals *Mystici Corporis* and *Mediator Dei*) and particularly the Second Vatican Council, were the first to seek to renew the link with the Aquinas synthesis. For example, the Constitution on the Church says that 'Acting in the person of Christ, the ministerial priest brings about the eucharistic sacrifice and offers it to God in the name of the whole people of God' (*Lumen gentium*, no. 10). Therefore, just as the Eucharist is Christ's gift to us and at the same time our offering to God, so also the priest is acting sacramentally in place of Christ and also in the name of the Church: he 'represents' Christ and represents the Church. But how is this 'and' to be more precisely understood?

2. A trinitarian concept of ministry

a) *The trinitarian dimension of the work of salvation* This brief examination of the history of theology has drawn attention to an extremely important dual aspect of church ministry which must be considered in greater depth. Ministry is the ministry of Christ and the ministry of the Church. What is the foundation and significance, what is the spiritual link, of this twofold relationship?

Attention has already been drawn to Christology. Two movements in opposite directions meet in Christ: he comes from the Father to us *and* he takes us with him on the way to the Father. The first movement corresponds within the Trinity to the procession of the Son from the Father. It is the movement of mission. A mission involves two pairs of contrasting opposites: on the one hand, the one who sends and the one who is sent; on the other hand, the one sent and the one to whom he is sent. The one who is sent receives mission and authority from the sender, but he must surrender himself in complete obedience to the mission he has been given. In the same way, Jesus Christ is sent by God into the world. From his Father he receives power and authority: to him he yields complete obedience. Consequently he is able to let the word and the love of God shine out for the men to whom he has been sent. 'He who sees me, sees the Father' (Jn 14:9). This mission of Jesus continues in a different but analogous manner on different levels — in the apostolic and post-apostolic ministry which is sent to the community, and in the Church as a whole which is sent to the world. The sending is marked throughout by obedient fulfilment of the mission given by the sender and by devoted service in working towards its goal.

But the sending of Christ is only one of the 'movements' which proceed from God. The Father does not only send the Son and give himself completely in him, giving through him his own heart, as it were (cf. Jn 1:18). He also sends the Holy Spirit, the Spirit of the mutual love of Father and Son, in order to draw all creation through him into the unity of the triune God. For this reason the sending of Christ cannot be separated from the action of the Spirit: it is in the Spirit that the Son of God enters history and becomes man (Lk 1:35); in him he carries out his messianic ministry of reconciliation and salvation (Lk 4:18); in his death on the cross he gives his Spirit for all mankind in order to join himself in him with all believers, into one body (1 Cor 12:12), a body which together with Christ offers itself to the Father in the Holy Spirit. Always and everywhere it is the Spirit who creates union, unity, community. This movement to *communio*, wrought by the Spirit, corresponds to the procession within the Trinity of the Spirit from the Father and the Son and their union in mutual love. Hence the characteristic element of Christ's mission: the authority (*exousia*) which his Father gave him, and which distinguishes him from men, is raised up into a greater unity (without simply disappearing as a result).[8]

The absolute 'priority' of Christ with respect to mankind, which is the basis of his uniqueness, is brought into a higher unity in the Holy Spirit: Christ becomes the principle of life for each believer and for his 'body' which is the Church. His word and salvation, his power and authority become interiorised, to such an extent that Christ's word and man's response of faith to it, Christ's salvific activity and the acceptance of sanctification, Christ's direction and guidance and the willing obedience of men: these coalesce into a complete unity, so that the believer can say 'I live, not I, but Christ lives in me' (Gal 2:20), and the Church becomes 'the fulness of him who fills the universe' (Eph 1:23). Therefore, from the christological aspect of Jesus Christ and his mission, the Church is the 'Bride of Christ', joined together by him into the *congregatio fidelium*, the faithful who orientate themselves on him, and — regulated so to speak from outside — allow his shape to be imprinted on them. Pneumatologically — that is, with respect to the creative and unifying activity of the Spirit — the Church is the 'body of Christ' and allows his majesty to shine forth and depicts him in his fulness (cf. Eph 4:13; 2 Cor 3:18).

Consequently, the people of God is, as it were, shaped by the 'objective form' of Christ and the 'interior life' of the Spirit, by the 'visible organised form' and the 'power of the Spirit'. The outward objective christological form communicates and supports the presence of the Spirit, and the Spirit labours to imprint on all the living the form of Christ. Form seeks to become life, life seeks to find form. The two aspects cannot be separated. They are no more inconsistent with each other than the Father, Son and the Holy Spirit. They demonstrate that the Church, because it is a creation of the triune God, is involved in a great trinitarian movement: it is the people of God the Father: he creates it through the Son in the Holy Spirit. As a result it is impressed with differing, and yet complementary, features.

b) *Church office as the intersection of authority (of Christ) and communio (of the Holy Spirit)* Priestly office also is marked by this trinitarian structure of the Church. Christologically, through mission and ordination, its purpose is to continue sacramentally the work of Christ in word, sanctification and teaching. Thus it is acting *in persona Christi* and represents the Lord of the Church to the rest of the baptised. Pneumatologically, on the other hand, the ministry, as the official organ of the Church, is central to its structure. As such it witnesses to the faith of the Church and demonstrates the priestly character of the whole people of God. It presides at the celebration of the liturgy, where the community extols the gifts of God which they have received, and it makes present the unity brought about in the Church by the action of the Spirit — the union of the members with one another and the union of all with Christ. From this point of view the priest is acting *in persona ecclesiae* and represents the Church before God and before the world.

If the ministry is understood solely from the christological aspect, it remains isolated under the sign of (Christ's!) authority and power. If it is conceived as exclusively pneumatological, it is *one* form of service among the other ministries in the Church which are the work of the Spirit. But since the Church is the indivisible work of the triune God, it is founded by the Father as one people, which is indeed one (in the Holy Spirit), and yet is so structured in its form that in this unity the priority of Christ, his word and his salvation become sacramentally perceptible.

Consequently, if church office is to be rightly understood, it must not be approached from Christ alone (which western theology tends to do)[9] nor from the charismatic community, the work of the Spirit (which is the danger for Reformation theology). It must be approached from the Father who sends Christ *and* the Spirit in inseparable unity to create the people. Through the united action of Christ and the Spirit, this people is, from the beginning and not merely subsequently, a unity, with the differentiation not only of ministers (that as well) but also of different 'orders'. In these 'orders' the office of the minister *as such* is to make the mission of Christ sacramentally present to the laity, while the laity witnesses to the reception of Christ's sacrificial action, makes effective its fruitfulness which is wrought by the Spirit, and transmits it to the Church and the world. Thus, regarded from the trinitarian aspect the Church subsists from the beginning in the unity and distinction of its 'ranks', however much this word may be liable to be misunderstood. What is true of Christ and his Church ('the body is the fulness of the head, and the head is the fulness of the body' (Chrysostom) is also true of the relation of the ministry to the community: it is only in their mutual distinction and complementarity that the 'fulness of God' is achieved.

Speaking formally, one can say: *in persona Christi* the priest represents the head of the Church; *in persona ecclesiae* he represents the body of Christ built up and filled by the Holy Spirit. Ordination, therefore, sets the office-bearer also in a twofold relationship — to Christ in whose name and by whose power he transmits the work of salvation to the people of God, and to the Church, whose faith he recapitulates, over whose celebrations he presides and whose unity he manifests. But this is if (and as long as) the Church knows itself to be *really* represented in the minister. This double character of the ministry accords with the earliest teaching of the Fathers. Congar has pointed out that one finds both aspects together in the writings of the Apostolic Fathers — 'unusually strong statements regarding hierarchy, and statements of the principle of community'. Although the ministry, to the extent that it represents the Church, essentially depends on the assent of the community, as representing Christ it is distinct from the rest of the faithful. Yet it is itself included in the *communio* and supported by it, since it cannot be effective except where it is recognised at least in general as a sacramental mediation of the reality of Christ. For this reason sacramental mediation is also only possible in the context of the life of the Church.

The following example can make this clear. The eye has for a human person the special and irreplaceable function of perceiving and transmitting reality. At the same time it is not the eye which sees, but it is the whole person who sees by means of the eye. If the eye is cut out, it is not longer any eye, an organ of sight, in the proper sense of the word. When the eye is separated from the organism, its specific essence is destroyed. Destroyed also is the whole organism, to the extent that it can no longer see. The specific essence of the eye 'consists in this, that it makes sight possible for the one who sees: in the act of seeing it does not itself see or be seen. The function of the eye is essentially mediatory. To the extent that it emerges as something separate and individual — when it is diseased — seeing becomes impossible: and when it is the only thing seen, then the one who sees ceases to exist as such, he is blind. The phenomenon of blindness is a state in which the eye has become the only thing seen. In this state it has come into total prominence and has set aside its essential function of mediation' (G. Pöltner). It is only in the totality of the organism that the organ can perform its official service of mediation. The connection with ministry in the Church is obvious. The ministry too can carry out its mediatory service *in persona Christi* only when it is not separated from the church organism, or when it does not make itself the object of its own attention but remains instead as a ministry of pure service in that organic unity which the Holy Spirit joins together and fills with life.

The Evangelical-Catholic dialogue of the Dombes Group on the subject of 'episcopal office' has very appropriately summarised the trinitarian structure of the ministry: 'The type of organisation in every community expresss the network of relationships existing in the community. The totality of the ministerial relationships in the Church must make clear the reception of the gifts of the Spirit, openness to the Lordship of Christ, and the filial adoration of the Father'. This plurality (= trinity) of aspects is actually expressed in the ministry of the Church: *in persona Christi* the ministry represents the saving Lordship of Christ; *in persona ecclesiae* it represents the reception of the gifts of the Spirit, and in and together with the rest of the community it devotes itself to the adoration of the Father. Since the two aspects of ministry, representation of Christ and representation of the Church, are mediated from the Trinity, it is ultimately not important for understanding them from which aspect one begins. If one starts with the first aspect, it must be immediately added that acting *in persona Christi* is possible and has meaning because Christ wishes to prepare a body for himself which through the fruitfulness of the Holy Spirit is open and ready for his action (mediated by the ministry). If one begins with the second aspect, one must add that the Church has nothing of itself but must accept the gifts of Christ and in the way in which he wishes — through the mediation of sacraments (including the ministry of the Church). Wherever one starts, it is a process of reciprocal mediation.[10] Just as Christ transmits the Holy Spirit, so also the Holy Spirit mediates the salvific action of Christ. Without the faith of the Church, the fruit of the Spirit, the priest would be completely unable to represent Christ, since his word and action presupposes faith and a corresponding interior consent. On the other hand, it is precisely through the sacramental mediation of Christ by the ministry that the Spirit finds the form and expression that are proper to him.

c) *Trinitarian tension and human contention*   Since under the aspect of trinitarian theology ministry and community are strictly related to one another in unity *and* difference,[11] this reciprocal relationship can take very different forms: it can even take the form of contention. In the context of our sinful existence and history, the growth of the faithful into becoming the body of Christ is no harmonious process of uninterrupted development. The interior spiritual readiness to accept Christ's gifts, transmitted through the ministry of the official Church, is often only partial, defective, and limited by sinfulness. For this reason the ministerial action 'in the name of Christ', through preaching, sanctifying and guiding, is not always responded to on the part of the community with willing and spontaneous acceptance in the Holy Spirit. On the contrary, it can happen that many Christians do not see the activity of the institutional Church as being the visible and objective form of the life of the Church, produced interiorly in the Holy Spirit. They see it instead as an alien authority and an irritant, which should be faced with protest, with disdain and with opposition.

It is certainly true in general that where a person happens to come into conflict with the exercise of external authority, he sees it at first as something strange and even hostile. Since this 'outside' force does not proceed from his own freedom, it appears as something limiting or even destroying his freedom. It is only when authority is understood, recognised and accepted that it is no longer felt to be something alien: because of interior acceptance, freedom can accept as its own what was at first 'outside' and hostile, and can form with it a *communio* of the 'other' and 'itself'. This is a general datum of anthropology and is also true of the relation of a (free) spirit and the external authority of the ministry.

Where the individual believer or the community understands and accepts that church office is the outward form of that liberating life to which the Spirit moves and urges interiorly, there can be no conflict between freedom and church authority. But what if the person refuses to give this inner consent? Then authority remains a mere claim, an undisguised demand. This happened already with Christ himself. He spoke with authority when he said, 'Repent'(Mk 1:15); with authority he issued his threat of the judgment (Mt 11:20ff); with authority he carried on the debate with the Pharisees. This conflict continued in the exercise of authority by the official church in apostolic and post-apostolic times. The office-bearer must proclaim not only God's mercy but also his demands, and therefore he meets with opposition from individual hearers, as well as from whole communities. In face of this, if authority in the Church resolutely carries out its assigned task, it becomes an authority which suffers. 'He who makes himself a teacher who tickles the ears [of his hearers] and substitutes fables for the Gospel [2 Tim 4:3] does not need to suffer for these fables. But he who holds fast to the Gospel, soberly, loyally and incorruptibly, must suffer for the truth of the Gospel and in this very way manifests its truth'. Readiness to suffer for the Gospel becomes 'the certificate and sign-manual of the preacher of truth' (G. Lohfink). There is consequently something profoundly personal involved in the 'official' character of the ministry: the one who must be a firm institution of 'power' for others is by this very fact called to give witness, by personal and living suffering.

But it is not only the community which can disturb the basic interrelation of the ministry and the community by refusing its consent to the action taken by the ministry as representing Christ. The office-bearer can also be the cause of profound conflicts. This happens when he carries out his office arbitrarily and autocratically, instead of giving Christ pride of place and serving the community: and also where he complacently sets himself over the community without troubling to win its understanding and consent, or to listen to it and learn from it. To put the point briefly: if the flock can no longer recognise in the minister the voice of the true shepherd, Christ, the priest is the cause of conflicts between the ministry and the community. Already in the Old Testament the judgment of God is proclaimed on the 'shepherds who feed themselves' (cf. Ezek 34:2), that is, who are concerned with themselves, their own advantage and power, and who misuse their authority over the flock. In the presence of false shepherds of this kind, as the past and present times show, the Church becomes the community of those who suffer under their office-bearers and on occasion finds them hard to endure; they do perhaps accept what the minister does officially, but they must reject his personal mode of official action and lifestyle.

In conflicts of this kind, the difference between the official Church and the community is not a reflection of their difference in rank, deriving from their relation to the Trinity. It is instead an expression of contradiction and opposition, and it shows that the growth process of the Church has become distorted. The inability to achieve harmony between the objective person of Christ, made sacramentally visible in the ministry, and the subjective life of the Church, which is the work of the Spirit, forces the official Church into pure officialdom, into a '*purely* juridical formalism which disguises and degrades its nature' (H. Urs v. Balthasar). This is a feature of the transitory and sinful nature of history which will one day disappear, as soon as the Spirit fills all and God is all in all.

Not only because of the conflicts mentioned, but also because of the differing standpoints which the community adopts in the process of the formation of the Church, the actual relationship between the official Church and the community can take on very different forms. In a living community which is full of the Spirit, the office-bearer can limit his mandate to act in place of Christ to the symbolical and sacramental representation of Christ, and in other respects regard himself much more as an organ of service to the community. In a 'dead' community, on the contrary, the aspect of mission with authority to begin by creating a community will be much more prominent. But both elements must always be preserved in carrying out the office: office is the office of Jesus Christ and the office of the Church.

d) *Office and the consent of the Church*   It is of course God himself who brings his people together in the Holy Spirit through Jesus Christ: but this does not happen without a corresponding consent on the part of men and women to become the body of Christ and to follow along his way together. It is in freedom that men offer to God the sacrifice of praise and self-devotion. Therefore the action of the priest, so far as he is acting *in persona Christi*, presupposes the faith and readiness of the individual to accept incorporation into the body of Christ through the priest — which means through the Lord himself. For this reason also, the authority of the official Church can be no other than that 'of the suppliant Christ' (E. Jüngel); it can and may fundamentally say no more than this, speaking as wooer and a suppliant, 'For Christ we beseech you, be reconciled to God' (2 Cor 5:20).

But the authority of church office presupposes not only basic agreement in faith, but also, to the extent that it is acting *in persona ecclesiae*, the consent of the faithful to having a *particular person* as office-bearer. In other words: since office (also) represents the Church, being a symbolical concentration and organ of action of the community, it needs the consent of the community which is joined together by the Holy Spirit. It is true that ordination means the 'taking over' of a man by Christ and so puts the one ordained in a position distinct from the rest of the community; but it is impossible for him to represent them officially and sacramentally without their consent. Both elements, representation of Christ and representation of the Church, affect one and the same person: consequently ordination and the exercise of office in virtue of ordination cannot take place without the consent of the Church.

From this, two conclusions of the historians of theology can be understood:

(1) There is a longstanding tradition in the Church that there are circumstances in which it can no longer be tolerated that a particular office-bearer should act in the name of the Church (although the Church cannot prevent him from continuing to act — perversely! — *in persona Christi*). For the medieval Church such circumstances were strictly limited and exceptional. There is no reason why the range of such cases should not be extended. At any rate the fact that the priest is also acting *in persona ecclesiae*

is accompanied by the conviction that this power is not permanently granted to him by ordination alone, but is subject to definite conditions set by the Church. It is only when the testimony of the Spirit in the Church agrees with the witness given by the office-bearer, that the 'flock' can recognise in it the voice of the 'shepherd' and follow him (Jn 10:4). For this reason office-bearers in the Church cannot act and ought not to act unless a certain minimum harmony exists or can be established between them and their fellow-Christians. The Church was completely convinced of this up to and during the Middle Ages. Cyprian can be quoted as one source among many others: 'Since the beginning of my episcopal office, I have made it my rule to take no decision according to my personal opinion, without listening to your advice and the voice of my people.'

(2) From ancient times, the rite of ordination is distinguished by two elements:

(a) The people of God present for ordination persons in whom they believe that they can discern, through the operation of the Spirit, the gift which makes them able to be shepherds and presiding officers.

In the early centuries it is often the local community which proposes its presiding officer. Indeed, according to some old canons, there is a prohibition on 'absolute ordinations', that is, ordinations without a connection with ministry in a concrete local church. For instance, canon 6 of the Council of Chalcedon: 'No one must be ordained absolutely: instead, a church (*ekklesia*) is to be distinctly assigned to him, in the city, in the country, or one dedicated to the memoria of a martyr or belonging to a monastery. If on the contrary he is ordained absolutely, the laying-on of hands on him is invalid, according to the decision of the holy Synod'. In the relationship to a community which is established together with the ordination, there is a clear indication that church office is nothing 'in itself' but is entirely 'for others'.

E. Schillebeeckx believes that this canon is the correct starting-point for arriving at the definition of ordination in the first Christian millenium. According to him, 'ordination is "incorporation" as office-bearer into a community, which calls a particular fellow-Christian and designates him as its presiding officer'. According to Schillebeeckx, this makes it clear that the office-bearer receives his authority to lead the community from the Holy Spirit *via the community* (through the laying-on of hands and *paraclesis*, invocation of the Holy Spirit). 'Only a person who is called by a particular community to be its presiding officer and leader may receive "ordination"'. The interpretation here given by Schillebeeckx to the sixth canon of Chalcedon clearly goes beyond the data, and is profoundly unhistorical. *Firstly*: nowhere does canon 6 say that the call and mission of the office-bearer are made through the community. *Secondly*: strictly canon 6 is not concerned with the relation of the office-bearer to the local community. Quarrels about jurisdiction and violent demonstrations of monks against the competent bishops are the real background of this canon. 'In view of these abuses and disorders, it was now important to strengthen the authority of the bishop over his clergy. The clergy were above all to be connected with a particular church, and to be under the higher authority of the bishop, even if they belonged to a monastery or to some other shrine' (P.-Th. Camelot).

Canon 6, therefore, does not deal with the theology of the relationship of a (local) community and the ministry, but with the legal position and subordination of the presbyter to the competent *bishop*. 'The Council was not dealing with our present problem, that someone from the community is presented for ordination: its concern was to bring under definite control clerics without a superior and a bishop' (J. Weismayer).

. Moreover, canon 6 proves just the *opposite* to what Schillebeeckx and others wish to prove: the priest is not primarily attached to a local *community* but to a *bishop*, who is the competent authority for one or more communities. Nevertheless, although canon 6 is to be interpreted otherwise than as Schillebeeckx does, it still remains true that in early times relative ordination (that is, ordination related to a definite community) seems to have been the norm. However, it was probably not the universal practice, probably not even originally. A more precise examination of the sources shows — as G. Kretschmar emphasises — that 'Christian ordination originally — if we may make use of the pastoral epistles — is not essentially in the first place aimed at making appointments to previously existing positions in the Church. In later times as well, this was not forgotten. In the early Church, and again in the Middle Ages, there was in addition to the local bishop, the missionary who was not elected by a community, but who instead first gathered his community together by his preaching. He also, like the community pastor, has the authority of mission. Here we have the justification for the practice which was initiated in the Middle Ages, and which became customary in modern times, of absolute ordination in the sense of not being related to one place.'

From the first epistle of Clement we learn of cooperation and consent of the community at the ordination of an office-bearer.

That does not mean that the candidate for ordination must be elected by a majority vote of a definite community. Moreover, it is 'not the community which appoints priests; this is the duty of bishops, who in this matter are the instrument of the Lord. But the community sees to it that it procures for itself the priests that it needs' (Y. Congar). For this reason, in the early Christian centuries communities did not hesitate to apply strong pressure to suitable men and to put it to them that they were needed as office-bearers (cf. p. 165 below).

There are many forms of the assistance and agreement of the community at the ordination of an office-bearer. Since the original choice of a person came widely under the influence of group interests and political power, the right of choice was more and more pushed into the background and eventually community involvement was reduced to an acclamation of consent, as in the Eastern Church the cry of '*Axios!*', or in the West a ratifying 'Amen'. Perhaps community cooperation at ordination has thus been reduced to a mininum: perhaps today we should be seeing new ways for the people of God to join in: certainly, the agreement of the Church is a *constitutive* part of the integral ordination rite.

The election or agreement of the community — the decision 'from below' — is a *manifestation* of the action of the Holy Spirit 'from above'. God issues his call in a human way: consequently the whole 'process' of an individual vocation is marked by multiple human mediation: through external impulses and interior aptitude, God causes the thought and wish to become a priest to arise in a Christian: he causes the charisma given to him to be verified by the community and moves the community to signify its readiness to accept the candidate as its office-bearer. Similarly, through admission to ordination by already ordained office-bearers, the sense of vocation of the candidate and the agreement of the community are as it were tested and brought into the specific christological relation. In this way the vocation 'process' culminates in the ordination which is the work of Christ. Therefore, the cooperation of the Church is an essential part of the 'process' of vocation: it is not something secondary. From early times, presentation by the community and its expression of consent are an 'organic part of the process which ends with ordination' (Y. Congar). It is not merely a piece of courtesy or just a ceremonial gesture: on the contrary, it is an expression of the inner trinitarian structure of the Church in which the christological and pneumatological movements interlock: the Spirit who is at work in the Church seeks as it were agreement with the outward form of the testimony of Christ, sacramentally represented in the official Church, while the official Church is bound, through the Holy Spirit, to the Gospel of Christ which is believed and practised in the Church. And perhaps much of contemporary dissatisfaction with ecclesiastical authority stems from the fact that the pneumatological and ecclesial dimension of the official Church, expressed in the agreement of the people, has become benumbed and reduced to a mere ceremony.

(b) When the community has signified assent to the ordination of a candidate, there comes the laying-on of hands by those who already share officially in the mission of Christ. As it has been previously explained in greater detail (pp. 53ff), the imposition of hands has two significances. *Firstly*, the ordaining prelates ask, with prayer and imposition of hands, for the sacramental completion by God of the spiritual gifts already tested in the candidate, and give him a guarantee of this completion in virtue of Christ's promise. In this way the ordained becomes a representative of Christ, his fellow-worker and sacramental sign. *Secondly*, the candidate is coopted into the college of bishops or presbyters, which is formally and materially in the unbroken line of succession to the apostolic college. He and the community through him are brought into the whole *communio* of the Church.

Ordination involves acceptance into that college which is conscious of its continuity with the apostolic Church — the guarantee of church unity-in-multiplicity. To that extent the office-bearer in his individual community represents the *communio ecclesiae catholicae*. He is its instrument and sign: that is, he has the duty to guide the community entrusted to him into the movement of unity with the whole Church. Nevertheless, this significance of the laying on of hands is not the only or even the principal aspect of ordination. Ordination is and remains primarily a sacramental granting of an ablity to represent Christ — an ability which presupposes that the Church is also willing to have the candidate for ordination as its own 'representative'.

The twofold character of the ministry — ministry of Christ and ministry of the Church — is also expressed in the twofold character of the ordination rite. Using the traditional terms, one could speak of the 'matter' and 'form' of the rite: the consent of the Church makes the candidate potentially a priest and able to receive the essential form of special mission and spiritual power from Christ (acting through commissioned officials). This twofold character is already implied in the Acts of the Apostles: 'Choose men from your midst . . . *we* shall appoint them to this task' (Act 6:3). The consent of the people makes the candidate for ordination a person suitable for acting in the name of the Church: the laying-on of hands takes possession of him through Christ for the mission. The Church must recognise in the activity of the ministry the priority of God's uncovenanted gift (the christological aspect), and also see that it is itself represented in the ministry (the pneumatological aspect). Only then will it will be able to perceive that it is a creation of the triune God — a creation in which office-bearers and layfolk are not separate parties but brethren with different tasks and 'roles'.

3. Ministry and charisma

The priest may be viewed christologically as acting in place of Christ or pneumatologically as acting in the name of the Church: in both these aspects he is an office-bearer: that is, his effectiveness is not attached primarily to him as a person but to his sacramental office. But since this office is one of mere mediation and thus points far beyond itself; still more, since it is (only) the christological mediation and outward structure of the divine life produced immediately in the faithful by the Holy Spirit, God and his activity are not 'channelled' and restricted to the official Church and what it does officially. On the contrary, the Spirit of God bestows on the faithful his multiple gifts and aptitudes (charismata), whose basic (and christological) form is indeed linked to official sacramental mediation, but whose fulness and fruitfulness are his covenanted and immeasurable gift. Thus the Spirit also gives rise to mission and new spiritual movements in the Church, which are not only not initiated by the official Church but often enough have to make headway against the resistance of church office-bearers. In this way the 'layman', that is each member of God's people, has in his individual life of faith and his mission for others, an independence before God, that is, a special vocation and an unique immediacy to God, which are not derived from the official Church.

It is altogether possible, and has very often happened in the history of the Church, that the preservation and safeguarding of the Church at a particular time, and the decisive spiritual impulse of a whole epoch, came about in the Church through charismatic lay people, not through the official Church. Think, for example, of the contrast between Innocent III and Francis. In Innocent we have church office, the official Church, in its full magnificence; in Francis, on the other hand, the little man, insignificant, a layman called by God. And yet: which of them had greater importance for the Church? Surely Francis! This contrast between official and lay person has often recurred in the Church and it is happening today too, even in the smallest communities. Often it is the lay person, and not the official Church, that supports and characterises the Church in its proper life. Thus the charismatic endowment of each one of the baptised reveals the office-bearer as one who receives, one who is in need, one who is essentially dependent on the whole people of God, in which the Holy Spirit is at work.

Yet, since in Christ God's salvation has definitively become 'flesh', that is, has taken a visible structure and unambiguous form, every spiritual gift, every individual testimony, every special vocation must fit in with the apostolic testimony which points to Christ, and to the way of the Church, a way which is based on the mission of the Apostles. It is only thus that the charisma is proved to be a fruit of the Holy Spirit and not a product of subjective caprice. Hence the value of the advice 'Test the spirits, and see if they come from God; for many false prophets have come out into the world. By this is the Spirit of God known: every spirit, which confesses that Jesus Christ is come *in the flesh*, is from God' (1 Jn 4:1f). That means: it is only when the 'charismatic' has shown through a process 'of discernment of spirits' that his charisma is genuine, that he has authority [to speak], it is only then that his gift is proved to derive from the Holy Spirit; only then has he significance in showing the Church the way. An essential part of this process is agreement with the 'flesh', that is, with the apostolic faith of the Church handed on and guaranteed by the official

Church.'If someone has the gift of prophecy, let him speak in agreement with the faith' (Rom 12:6). Looked at in this way, the official Church, which has to give testimony of the word of God with power and authority, is *one* criterion of the genuineness of the charismata (which it has not produced and which it has not to administer).

But when a charisma has been shown to be a gift of the Holy Spirit, then it comes before the whole Church (including the ministry) with a comprehensive claim to be heard: it can claim to be accepted and obeyed. One need only think of the great saints among the laity, and their mission in the Church. Still more: just as a charismatic who has been tested and proved can speak 'in the name of Christ', so also can the 'Church of the Spirit' be represented in him. Indeed one must agree that 'For the Fathers of the Church, the "men of the Spirit", the martyrs, the ascetics and the saints were the ones in whom, especially and above all, the Church was crystallised' (Y. Congar). But this charismatic 'representation' does not contradict the sacramental action of the official Church; it presupposes it. The charismatic element must be incorporated into the christological structure of the Church, the structure mediated and guaranteed by the official Church in virtue of the effective promise made by Christ. It is only then, and to that extent, that the movement can produce the fullness of Christ, the fruitfulness and holiness of the Church which is the work of the Spirit. Thus it can often do much more than the official Church, which is not infrequently humbled by the holiness of the laity and is itself drawn to holiness by being humbled in this way.

Thus here also it becomes clear once more that the official Church and the rest of the faithful who are endowed with charismata are strictly related to one another — by unity and by contrast. Augustine's description of this 'dialectic' is well known: 'When I am frightened by what I am for you, I am consoled by what I am with you. For you, I am a bishop, with you I am a Christian. The former designates an office, the latter, grace. The former spells danger, the latter, salvation'. J. Ratzinger comments: 'Each Christian, regarded individually, and in himself alone, is only a Christian and cannot be anything higher. The one name of Christian is unique and indivisible. In himself — *ad se* — each one is simply a Christian and that is his dignity. *Pro vobis*, that is in relation to the others, a relation which is irrevocable and which touches the one concerned in his whole being, a man becomes an office-bearer. Office and relation coincide: the office is the relation *pro vobis*, for you'. Concluding his commentary Ratzinger says: 'There is no need to stress the demand which this understanding of church office makes on the holder of that office.'

PART TWO

The spiritual life of the priest

4

The basis of the priest's spiritual life

1. The centre of the priest's life

Since according to Scripture and Tradition the priest is a representative, deputy and outward form of Jesus Christ, and since his office is founded on a special mission from the Lord of the Church, this office-bearer must also set his course towards Jesus Christ and take him as a standard. Christ is the prototype of all priesthood.

The first consequence of this is a negative one. It is misleading to couple the priesthood, its essence, significance and content, with other 'similar' vocations, or to use them as a standard of measurement and comparison. One often finds a tendency to do this in what are called 'progressive' church circles. An attempt is often made to relate priestly activity to other 'socially relevant' vocations, or to put it on their level. The priest then takes his place among social workers, adult educators, teachers, health visitors, youth leaders, psychologists, prophetic critics of society, as a functionary whose job is to satisfy people's sense of religion and transcendence, and as an expert in theology. This tendency (here slightly caricatured) derives from a feeling of concern which has to be taken seriously. When asked, 'What exactly are you? What exactly is your work?', the priest would like to be able to point to something socially plausible, something accepted and relevant. He would like people to realise that the priesthood of the Church is something of the greatest importance for mankind. But the priest of today may perhaps have to accept that his calling no longer holds, as once it did, a definite, recognisable and generally accepted place in our society, and a corresponding social prestige. Did Jesus then have a definite, recognisable and generally accepted position? Did his mission not involve his being homeless, his not receiving universal recognition, but instead meeting with opposition and not fitting in with the social structure of the time (cf. Mt 8:20)?

If Jesus Christ is the standard and prototype of priestly office, it is necessary to inquire into the central feature of his life and mission. He was the 'Man for others' — an expression of D. Bonhoeffer which is often and rightly used today. He was totally the 'man for others' surrendering himself in the service of his brethren. But this he was in such a way that he was simply 'God's man' — to use a biblical expression. He was there for men, because he was there for God, and obediently accepted his mission from God to save mankind. Thus, he was able to announce to them God's forgiveness and love, to pass on to them confidence, courage and hope, to gather them together into the 'family of God', the community of his brothers and sisters (cf. Mt 12:29), which is ready to receive ultimate salvation from God. The fact that Jesus has come from God on our behalf is biblically expressed in the announcement of the imminent coming of God's kingdom. When Jesus proclaimed that 'the time is fulfilled, the kingdom of God is at hand', he meant that in him God was now coming in to the world, to impart to it his definitive love. This coming of God is central to the life and mission of Jesus. His decisive achievement for mankind was not communication of knowledge about life, sensitivity training, social reform, organisation of works of charity; it was not the establishing of a religious service station, or the satisfying of human religious instincts. For him the central point was far more the coming of God's kingdom, the promise and the actual mediation of the Father's love which encompasses and transforms the whole world. He sought to prepare — even to 'break open' — mankind for this love and thereby give men a sense of fulfilment in life and a hope of achieving perfection. Thus, this 'last ambassador' of God has effectively manifested the 'total otherness' of God and his supremacy in a world which shuts out the love of the Father, a world satisfied with itself and therefore again and again falling into despair and suffocating itself: and he has done this by a message of forgiveness, love and consolation, especially through concrete signs of hope (driving out demons, healing the sick, helping the needy and the lonely), signs in which the dawn of the kingdom is already becoming visible.

His death on the cross also bears the signature of the coming kingdom: as the 'suffering servant' he takes the place which we on account of our sins should occupy, and takes us up into his attitude of radical obedience, unprotesting self-surrender and total trust in the love of the Father. Therefore, nothing can again 'separate us from the love of God' (Rom 8:39), which was promised to us in his Resurrection and which allows us to have a sure hope of the ultimate and definitive coming of the kingdom. The murder of his beloved Son was not able to destroy God's love for us, and now nothing can revoke his fidelity to his promise.

This mission of Jesus, to prepare and open up to the world for the coming kingdom of God, must be continued in the Church: in fact, the Church as a whole is charged with continuing the mission of Jesus by following in his footsteps. Therefore, as we have seen, there is a need for men who, representing him and with a commission from him, are willing to be sent in his name to proclaim the word of the kingdom and the message of God's 'foolish' love. By a sacramental rite they are to pass on the reconciliation which has been accomplished in him, and the irrevocable alliance of God with men founded on the death and Resurrection of Jesus. As pastors they are to issue a call to follow him, to gather and lead a community: as organs of God's people (*in persona ecclesiae*) by their ministry they are to make possible and to support the life of the Church before God and before the world. In a word: there is a need of men who will 'equip the rest of the faithful to fulfil their service, for the building up of the body of Christ' (Eph 4:12). But the purpose of all their ministry is to free the world from the self-satisfaction and narrowness of sin, and to prepare it for, to open it up to, and unite it into the kingdom of God.

A commitment of this kind to the kingdom of God is foolishness and a stumbling block in the eyes of a sinful world (1 Cor 1:23). Priestly office is a *spiritual* ministry which cannot be fulfilled except by a *spiritual* man. 'Such a man does not regard what is visible, manageable, calculable as the sole reality. He makes room for the free, uncovenanted action of the Spirit of God, and lives from the freedom of that Spirit' (W. Kaspar). Yet inasmuch as the kingdom of God and the activity of the spirit go beyond the dimensions of the immediate situation, spiritual ministry is not purely spiritual:

it is concerned with setting up in this world, here and now, visible signs of the kingdom, signs by which the coming sovereignty of God is sketched out in anticipatory outline. Such signs are to some extent concrete, visible, 'corporal'.

At particular times and in particular situations these signs may certainly take the form of youth work and social work and work to relieve human needs and cares. Jesus also healed the sick, fed the hungry, consoled the lonely, called men together out of their isolation into a community. But this he did not do in order to make the world better 'in itself' and thus endorse it 'in itself': through healing, helping and consoling he has established signs of hope which make credible the announcement of the kingdom of God, which breaks through the limits of the world. In the same way the spiritual ministry, as part of the community and forming with the community 'God's model society' (N. Lohfink), is called upon to set up for the world the signs of the kingdom which can bring about mutual reconciliation among men, enabling them to live in mutual love, brotherly peace and shared joy, in the expectation of ultimate happiness.

Just as the kingdom of God was central to the person and mission of Jesus, so it must be the centre of the priest's life and of his ministry. The office-bearer in the Church, by following Jesus, is first and last 'God's man' for mankind. He is deeply stirred by the kingdom of God and is specially committed to its service. He accepts a mission from Christ, his friend, and extends the kingdom on his behalf. 'You are my friends, if you do what I command you. I will not call you servants, because the servant does not know what his master is doing. But rather I have called you friends, for I have made known to you all the things which I have heard from my Father. You have not chosen me: but I have chosen you; and have appointed you that you should go and bring forth fruit, and that your fruit should remain'(Jn 15:14ff). Mission is personal admission to a share in the work of God and Christ.

2. Office and holiness

a) *Character indelebilis: the unchanging promise of God and a sign of human lowliness* Since priestly office is a sign and instrument of the Lord, present and effectively acting in his Church, it has the same centre and aim as Christ's own person and work — the kingdom of God. This is true in the first place of priestly office only in its objective sacramental essence — that is, insofar as its action is something institutional and more than individual, a sign which points to and mediates Christ's work of salvation, and which does not attach to the priest as an individual, to his achievements, his talents, his personality (cf. pp. 61ff). We have already seen that it is precisely the objective nature of the office that brings about the union of the community not with the office-bearer but with the Lord. Just as the glass windows in a house are not an intrusion between the sunlight and the room, but are a transparent medium making possible a meeting of the brightness of the day and the darkness inside, so also the priest is not a sort of 'relay' interposed between God and his people: 'on the contrary, his mediating office brings about an immediate mutual relationship. But this is possible only because the office-bearer has received a power from Christ, which enables him to act on Christ's behalf and to represent him sacramentally. This power is not attached to the personal action of the priest, but to his office, to his calling, his ordination, his mission.

In the Church, this power given in ordination is traditionally called a *character indelebilis* — an indelible stamp. It is indelible because it is effected by the unbreakable promise and unchanging will of Christ to transmit his work of salvation through the ministry of the ordained. The power to exercise the official ministry comes from God himself, according to what Paul says: 'Not that we are sufficient to think anything of ourselves, as if we could attribute anything to ourselves: our sufficiency comes from God, who has made us fit ministers of the New Testament, not of the letter, but of the spirit'(2 Cor 3:5f). Consequently, human sins and failures cannot frustrate and destroy this power. The 'character', therefore, does not establish an 'undue preferential position of the priest before the community, but means in the first place that his official actions do not ultimately depend on his personal situation before God with regard to his own salvation' (*Letter of the German Bishops*, 1969).

E. Dassmann points out that already in the early Church, the great

lay theologians had noticed and spoken about the discrepancy between
the deficiency of personal spiritual qualities in the bishop or priest and
their spiritual ministry. Thus, he says that in the opinion of Origen
'arrogance and pride . . . [are] typical qualities of clerics, as well as their
failure themselves to practise what they preach to the faithful according
to the Gospel. People of modest position and no culture often have a
perfection which is wanting in bishops and priests'. It is just in this
way that it becomes abundantly clear that the spiritual ministries of the
office-bearers are far beyond their human capacity, and simply 'cannot
be carried out unless the Church by conferring the office in ordination
is able to guarantee the assistance of the Holy Spirit.'

If the ministry of salvation depended upon personal holiness,
not only would the priest be completely overstretched, but the
eschatological and final offer of salvation, made by God in Jesus
Christ, would be limited by the sin and weakness of men, and
its ultimate validity would be open to question. The doctrine of
the indelible character is therefore not a declaration that the office-
bearer is superior to the lay person: it is instead the condition which
makes it possible for the Church to rely confidently on Christ's
promise in spite of the sins and shortcomings of office-bearers:
he himself is close to his Church in the actions of those whom
he has commissioned. For the office-bearer, however, the 'character'
conferred in ordination is a 'sign of lowliness', which should be
a constant reminder that he has not the power to destroy Christ's
work and the existence of his Church. In fact, it is this character
which first and foremost makes it possible 'to undertake
ecclesiastical office without presumption, but also without anxiety
and embarrassment' (E. Dassmann). It is ordination, i.e. the grant
of power through Christ, which gives that holiness which is
required for priestly action. Looked at in this way priestly office
which comes from Christ is something 'objectively holy' and
'objectively sanctifying' and in its official sacramental functions
it represents Christ and does not depend on the personal holiness
of the minister.

It was Augustine, particularly, who in the Donatist controversy
of the fourth and fifth centuries stressed the fact that the official
acts of an office-bearer derive their effectiveness from Christ, even
if the office-bearer lacks personal holiness. With endless variations
Augustine emphatically cites the example of Baptism: it does not

matter whether John or Judas baptises; it is always the baptism of *Christ*.'Those whom a drunkard baptised, or a murderer, or an adulterer — it is Christ who has baptised them, since it was the baptism of Christ. I do not fear the adulterer, the drunkard, the murderer, since I look at the Dove [= the Catholic Church], through which I am told, "This is the one who baptises."'[12] In other words: as a result of ordination it is Christ himself who is acting in the person of his minister, even when the one who has received ordination does not live in a manner which corresponds to what he does officially.

b) *'Imitate the things you handle'*　This outcome of the Donatist controversy has been called one of the 'most necessary' and at the same time 'most fateful' decisions of the Church. There is some truth in this. This decision was *necessary*: it made clear that the community was not dependent on the individual personality or personal holiness of the office-bearer, but on the power handed on to him by his ordination, and that means ultimately *by Jesus Christ himself*. But this decision was fateful, because it involved the danger of a choking functionalism and unbearable papal tyranny. Still more: it runs the risk of obscuring an essential feature of the revelation message. Scripture shows in many ways that whenever God takes men into his service and entrusts tasks to them, whenever his word seeks to appear to mankind, it is not only the individual acceptance of the person called that is required; that person is also asked to adopt a lifestyle in which his recruitment into God's service becomes sacramentally visible and is thus seen to be credible. A few pointers to this: since Abraham was to be a 'blessing for all generations' (Gen 12:2), and since he and his descendants were promised 'a city with strong walls, planned and built by God himself' (Heb 11:10), he had to leave his home in faith, and set out into darkness. He became a stranger without a home. It is in this way that the call he received took visible form. Moses and the prophets further develop this unity of vocation and witness of lifestyle: 'To them were entrusted the word and instruction of God — but in such a way that they must endure in their own bodies the complete defiance of them by the stiffnecked people: more exactly, that they must demonstrate how this contradiction affects God. We find God's wish "to strike the

Shepherd" (Zech 13:7) verified ever since the time intermediaries appeared in the Old Testament' (H. Urs v. Balthasar). Their vocation puts its stamp on their life, even in the most personal and intimate way (the marriage of Hosea; Jeremiah's fate and his renunciation of marriage, joy in life, success; the suffering of the Servant of God; the ascetic life of the Baptist). How could it be otherwise with Jesus! In him we find the most perfect unity of mission and life. The supremacy of God — the centre of Jesus' mission and activity — is as it were reality in himself 'before' he brings it to mankind. Origen calls Jesus Christ simply the *'autobasileia'*: the kingdom of God in person. He is what he does and he does what he is. In his life he is the union of sign and reality, of witness and testimony.

This unity must be continued in the life of the office-bearer in the Church. One who has the office of passing on the salvation of God's kingdom must be possessed and affected by it in his own person. This is particularly obvious in Paul, the model and type of church office, the model 'official' or office-bearer of the official Church. For him, it is simply a matter of fact that the Cross and Resurrection (that dual event which is the dawning of God's kingdom) must be put in practice in his own life prior to being proclaimed to others and proposed to the community: 'always carrying about in the body the death of Jesus, that the life of Jesus also may be manifested in our body. For we who live are constantly being delivered over to death for the sake of Jesus, that the life of Jesus also may be manifested in our mortal flesh'(2 Cor 4:10f). That means: Cross and Resurrection, the centre of Paul's apostolic activity, must become the fundamental principle of his own life, and must become visible in him. For this reason Paul does not merely proclaim the Gospel: he exemplifies it in his whole life. For this reason also he can say to the communities: 'Be followers of me, as I am of Christ' (1 Cor 11:1) — a command often repeated in various ways.

In the Apostle's lifestyle the community has before its eyes a concrete model of its Christian life, which results from imitation of Christ and expectation of the coming kingdom. Christ is, so to speak, shown and held up before it in the personal life of the Apostle. This does not mean merely moral exemplarity; Paul points candidly to the weakness, suffering and contradiction experienced in his apostolic life, since in the endurance of adversity both the form of Christ crucified and the reality of his hidden risen life become visible. Thus Paul presents himself before the community as the 'prototye of the action of God's grace on mankind' (G. Lohfink).

It becomes clear that 'the objective-sacramental and the subjective-existential elements are nowhere separable in the Church. The word of God, addressing man, requires the answer of man in order to be able to reach him at all: and the clearer the answer, the more profoundly the word of God enters into him. The objective-sacramental element is the making of God's love in Christ present for a particular community or individual or for a particular situation. The presence of this love is guaranteed by Christ's promise and also by the presence of the ministry in the Church: but it demands that the grace be consciously realised by those who receive it' (H. Urs v. Balthasar). It would therefore be a perversion, a reversal in the truest sense, to be an official sacramentally reprenting Christ, and perhaps to claim this as much as possible on the strength of being ordained, while on the other hand regarding personal representation (i.e. the formation of one's own life after the model of Christ), as something possibly pious and edifying, but still an optional extra. No: without a corresponding personal practice the ordained priesthood becomes a religious bureaucracy, fruitless, abstract, lifeless, which is not surprising: an office-bearer who does no more than the bare discharge of his official duties is a *monstrum*, an 'impossible possibility'.[13]

For example: when the priest at every Mass says 'This is my Body, which will be given up for you', he is speaking these words *in persona Christi*, in place of Christ, or, more correctly, Christ speaks them through him. And yet it is the priest who utters these words. Christ's word is transmitted through the word of the priest. Can, may, this word be no more than a ritual sacramentally official utterance? This might suffice for objective salvific validity. Yet Christ wishes to be seen in his completeness as a person. And consequently the words 'This is my Body which will be given up for you' must also become the personal words of the priest, in the sense 'Here is my body, i.e., my person, my life, which I give up with and in Christ for you, brethren, as your priest and pastor.'

When the words of consecration are not spoken in this sense also, there is a grating contradiction between official sacramental action and personal life.

This contradiction is the 'occupational hazard' of the office-bearer, and it is the first and fundamental task of the priest to overcome it. He must therefore, first of all, strive in his following of Christ to be a 'man of God' as described in the 'ordination sermon' of 1 Tim 6:11: that is, he must ensure that his life belongs to God and that God's kingdom has the first place in it.

This existential demand on the disciple with a particular mission becomes particularly clear in the numerous vocation texts in the Gospels (especially Mt 10:5ff.; 8:18f.; 16:24ff.). These demonstrate what Jesus expects from those whom he chooses to send to preach the kingdom. The essential point is that the disciple who is commissioned should, like Jesus, show visibly in this world by his personal life and mode of living the beginning of God's kingdom and its 'complete otherness'. For this reason, the disciple must be different, must maintain an 'alternative lifestyle'; he must leave everything behind and set out on his way without power and money; he must be poor and available and must set up a sign of peace and reconciliation. It is precisely in this way that he will become a sign of God's supremacy which in its otherness exposes the standards of this world. In what other way can the supremacy of God be credibly proclaimed, if the messenger does not seek to make it actual in his own life? If he is no more than a religious bureaucrat, his words and his actions are not credible, cannot touch the heart.

Since the disciple is sent 'to where the Lord himself wishes to come' (cf. Lk 10:11), the priest cannot carry out his mission if he is not permanently filled and touched by Jesus Christ. He must be one who before everything else listens to God: how else would he bring the will of God to men? He must be one who himself is a follower of Christ and is like him penetrated by the love of God: how else would he be able to invite others to follow, and how could he credibly communicate God's love? He must be one who himself has a radical hope and relies on God's new world: how else could he arouse in men a hope of the kingdom of God? Consequently, the priest not only *has* an official mission, but he *is* also personally called to make God's kingdom the centre of his life and to follow the way of Jesus with special earnestness, radically and visibly.

This unreserved commitment is a continual adventure, a journey into the unknown, something which strictly speaking demands 'all or nothing'. In his exposition of New Testament discipleship, D. Bonhoeffer has very clearly pointed to the temptation to turn discipleship into something entirely visible, commensensical and easy to understand: 'Suppose the disciple makes himself available but reserves a right to set out his own conditions. Obviously at this point following ceases to be following, for when God's call comes to man, only an unreserved consent is possible. Certainly God does not extinguish the smoking flax, as the Scripture says: yet he is a consuming fire that wishes to take hold of everything. Consequently, what Kierkegaard says is true: 'To seek close union with God in any other way than by being wounded is ... impossible.... One who seeks union with God without total surrender does not achieve it. In relationship with God it is impossible to seek union to a certain extent only, since he is the very opposite of everything that is limited in degree.'

If, therefore, the priest is a 'man of God' and if personal following of Christ and being possessed by the kingdom of God belong to his office, then there is inherent in him an impulse towards radicalism which persists in all the concrete details of his life. Wherever this radicalism is moderated and adulterated for any worldly reason, the priest's office will be less effective and less credible. Finally, it is no coincidence that in St John's Gospel, in which the handing over of the pastoral office   to Peter stands as a model for all transmission of office, the love of God is named as the one condition: 'Do you love me more than these?' (Jn 21:15). Significantly, no question is asked about readiness for self-sacrifice for the sake of mankind, but for Christ: since it is only from this that that self-sacrifice can arise whereby Christ the Shepherd gave himself up for the flock and which he expects from the disciples he has commissioned.

In these ways Holy Scripture gives many indications that only a union of vocation and lifestyle, a mutual interpenetration of the objective sacramental holiness of the office and personal holiness, can meet the requirements of priestly ministry. When Francis de Sales says that 'the difference between the written word of the

Gospels and the life of the Saints is the same as the difference between a musical score and its performance', this means that the priest should not merely pass on the score but must also take part in the performance, and in fact must be himself a 'hymn'.

c) *Holiness, a ministry for others*   There is something more: modern man is particularly sceptical about objective norms and claims based on formal and official authority, inherited institutions and traditional rights. He is very ready to see official transmission of the mystery of Christ as a well disguised ideology of domination, a dogmatically obscure sacramentalism, a clerical device to cramp his style. Behind this scepticism there is a profound and serious matter of concern: modern man is filled with a consciousness of freedom and can only experience 'objective' authority as something significant and full of meaning when he discovers in it the very 'form' of freedom, or — to put it in another way — when he discovers the spirit in the letter, personal commitment in the objective signs, unselfish spirit of service in the official authority; in short, when he can perceive actual commitment in the way in which the official institution operates.

The present-day widespread criticism of church authority claims to be 'scientific' by using an elaborate apparatus of historical criticism to interpret dogma and sociology. Yet how much it ultimately derives from personal disappointment and from real inability to experience (objectively holy) authority in a context of committed holiness! To cope with this difficulty the office-bearer has an obligation not merely to act 'officially' in place of Christ but also to do this in such a way that the salvific work of Christ can reach men through him as a real offer which effectively makes them free. For this it is necessary that the office-bearer should, as was said as early as the epistle to Titus (1:7), 'as God's steward be above reproach'. But it is necessary above all that the priest should be the first to be affected personally and that his mode of life should be marked by imitation of Christ and the coming of the kingdom. It is true that the objective effectiveness of his teaching, administration of the sacraments and guidance of the community does not depend on his living personally as one who believes, hopes and loves: but nevertheless it is only a priest of this kind who in the long run can guarantee that the objective communication of salvation will achieve its goal. It is only when the will of the hearer is alerted and open that the word will be accepted with belief, the sacraments will be fruitfully celebrated and preaching will be heard with interior consent. Therefore, the person empowered to perform priestly actions has the 'right and duty to bring about that context of the preaching of the faith' in which alone the objective sacramental action can find that 'disposition' or 'situation' in which 'it can actually be accepted with faith, and in which it can be effective' (K. Rahner).

The 'holiness' of the priest is consequently in a certain way incorporated in the 'motive of credibility' of the hearer. Spirit catches fire from spirit, faith is kindled by one who believes, imitation of Christ is stimulated by a disciple who is already imitating him, and freedom can be achieved only by the experience of freedom. Consequently, there is an 'ultimate inseparability of church office and actual mode of life' (K. Rahner). One who asserts that the priest is indeed called to holiness, 'but not to any other holiness than any other believer' (F. Haarsma), overlooks not only the unity of mission and personal testimony, a unity attested and proposed in Scripture, but overlooks also the actual situation today, which more than ever before requires a personal and credible preaching of salvation. For this reason the priest is indeed not called to a *greater* holiness: but his concern to achieve the unity of his official mission and his personal holiness is the specific *motivation* and consequently a *specific form of his spirituality*.

d) *Lifelong* This unity of office and personal life, of 'objective' and 'subjective' holiness, is also the fundamental reason why priestly office must set its mark on the whole of the priest's life, not merely in all its aspects, but also throughout its whole length. G. Bachl says rightly that 'if we are speaking about sacrifice and commitment, what other more important thing can one sacrifice and commit than one's time? And if the sacrifice and commitment are to be radical and total, how can this be truly possible if one's whole lifetime were not to be included. The value we set upon time can be seen in all spheres of human experience — from "Time is money" to "I can spare you some time" —, in many different situations trivial and important, but which all indicate that the person is administering a piece of capital by which he sets great store and which he economises in all sorts of subtle ways. Undoubtedly it is in this aspect of his life that a man is challenged when he is called upon to offer his life by Christian preaching: the sacrifice is essentially a sacrifice of his time'.

How can radicalism in time show itself otherwise than by a radical sacrifice of time? In this connection J.B. Metz' assertions are valid for every radical commitment, for every decision about life: 'A decision cannot be changeable as often as one pleases, if it is not to reveal itself once again as temporary and trivial, if it is not once again to be submerged in that ceaseless vacillation which is supposed to be ended by a responsible decision. For this reason a decision essentially tends to be once and or all, irreplaceable and irrevocable'. This is true of every real decision about life: but it is especially true when it is a decision about a mission from God and readiness to serve him. Already in the time of the Old Testament prophets, God 'takes over' the life of the one he calls, so that the one called cannot escape from his vocation (cf. Jer 20:7ff). This is particularly true of the priestly ministry which has to make present the self-sacrifice of Jesus for mankind; this can credibly happen only when the priest realises that he has been chosen and called to sacrifice all his strength and the whole time of his life. Thus, a priest's vocation is essentially a lifetime vocation.[14]

The unity of official position and holiness, of objective ministerial action and personal life, which is required of the priest, may at certain times in the history of the Church have receded considerably into the background and become obscured. Yet the demand for it has always been there. For this reason the Church has from the beginning set criteria for ordination candidates — criteria which make it possible to discern if the future office-bearer has a call from God, possesses the necessary spiritual gifts and is really ready to devote his entire life to the priestly ministry. As early as the first epistle to Timothy (5:22) Paul says, 'Do not impose hands on any man too hastily', that is, without a previous testing, a procedure for which the pastoral epistles set forth a series of criteria. These criteria serve in the first place to give the Church greater certainty: but they can also help the candidate to test the authenticity of his vocation and measure his readiness for the priestly ministry.

Among these criteria, as is well known, is celibacy. This will be discussed in detail in the next chapter: but it may be pointed out here that at no time was anyone called to an office in the Church without being subjected to criteria which at times impinged profoundly on the personal life and indeed the 'human rights' of the office-bearer (cf. 1 Tim 3:2-13; Tit 1:6-9). If, for example, according to 1 Tim 3:2 — at least as interpreted and applied by the Churches of the East for many centuries — it was among other things demanded of a bishop that he 'be married only once', this demand went against the 'worldly right' then existing to a second marriage, just as today the law of celibacy goes against the 'right to marry'. The line of argument against celibacy, widespread particularly in the sixties, alleging that it was contrary to human rights, is strictly speaking equally applicable to a whole series of other clear biblical preconditions for discipleship.

This unity of mission and personal life means in practice: *firstly*, that the model of the priest's life is that of the special imitation of Christ demanded of the disciples; *secondly*, that his objective and sacramental representation of Christ must take the form of humble service; and *thirdly*, that his life is lived in a tension between being part of and being distinct from the community. We will go on now to examine this threefold structure of priestly spirituality more closely.

5

Imitation of Christ in practice

What the imitation of Christ involves cannot be something thought out for oneself or something which one personally arranges and determines according to one's own ideas. The particular imitation proper to the disciples, to which Jesus Christ himself calls not everyone but only a few, has a prescribed form, a form already distinctly recognisable in the Gospels (cf. e.g. Lk 9:37ff; Mk 10:29ff). This 'form' can be summarised in its three fundamental features — poverty, obedience and celibacy. These are not three isolated and clearly separate styles of life, but three crystallisations of one life of special imitation of Christ. If we now begin with celibacy, it is not because it is the most important of the three evangelical counsels — that would be poverty — but because celibacy has a special importance as being one of the conditions for ordination in the Western Church and for this reason is today a matter of some controversy.

1. The evangelical counsels

a) *Celibacy*   Christ was not married. This did not happen fortuitously; in fact, it was contrary to Jewish custom. According to St Matthew's Gospel, Jesus recommended his celibacy to others and explained its significance: 'There are also eunuchs who have made themselves eunuchs for the sake of the kingdom of heaven. He who is able to accept this, let him accept it' (Mt 19:12). The celibacy of Jesus is therefore oriented towards the kingdom of God. Consequently, the disciples whom he appoints to the special service of the kingdom must leave everything — wife, children, father and mother. Thus, 'in the synoptic Gospels there is a profound link

THE EVANGELICAL COUNSELS 121

between the leaving of possessions and family on the one hand, and the service of the Gospel on the other. Jesus was unmarried, not for convenience, not because he disdained sexuality, but because he was most profoundly fascinated by the kingdom of God and filled by it' (G. Lohfink). He also calls disciples to share in this 'fascination'.

It is true that the second half of v. 12 indicates that not all 'accept' — that is, understand and put into practice — this invitation. In fact, celibacy for the sake of God's kingdom is ultimately based on God's free call, which man cannot produce in himself by argument.

Paul develops the saying related in St Matthew when he says, 'I wish that all men were [unmarried] even as I myself am. However, each man has his own gift from God, one in this manner, and another in that' (1 Cor 7:7). To be unmarried is a special gift of grace, since 'one who is unmarried is concerned about the things of the Lord, how he may please the Lord: but one who is married is concerned about the things of the world, how he may please his wife. And so he is divided' (1 Cor 7:32).

What is meant by this 'concern' for the things of the world, this being 'undivided', can be illustrated by the following passage from Heinrich Spaemann: 'I have been taken into the service of the fire. It is more important than anything else that I should catch fire. This means in practice that I should preserve my time, my heart and my life free and undivided for the revealing and redeeming word of the Lord, so that it comes first to me, so that I am myself the first to live according to it, and make it concrete, illustrating it by my own life and so proclaiming it to others. And surely that is the meaning of my celibacy — to keep alive the burning expectation of a reality which surpasses all the transient happiness which can be experienced in this world: and that I do this with total availability for those fellow-men to whom I must make this reality clear and with whom I must share it. I do not know them in advance: I do not know the full reach of that net of loving relationships which I must construct and cast out. This, to be sure, is or ought to be in the first place my parish: but essentially there is no limit. A bond with a natural family, with wife and children, would from the start mean a limitation, because it sets up a prior claim with all the consequent responsibilities which that imposes on me'.

Celibacy thus understood is in no way based on an expectation of the imminent approach of the kingdom of God, and particularly not in St Paul's teaching (as is often claimed). As K. Niederwimmer points out, it is particularly the Apostle who proposes it as 'that form of Christian life in which obedience to the Kyrios can be more perfectly practised. The one who belongs to the Kyrios (and that is after all the decisive element of Pauline Christianity) must belong to him entirely: and one who belongs to him entirely cannot also belong to another. In this sense the life of celibacy is that in which the newly-won freedom is better realised.' This interpretation comes from an Evanglical exegete who is beyond suspicion; it may displease many contemporaries, but it is just as displeasing when applied to the challenging attitude of Jesus himself and his challenging demand on the disciples. K. Niederwimmer also points out that, in view of this argument for an unmarried life, the real problem for the early Church was not celibacy, but marriage (just as in the same way it was not poverty but riches that were the problem).

Nevertheless, one would completely misunderstand celibacy for the sake of God's kingdom if one were to downgrade marriage or reckon it of little value. On the contrary: only a person who experiences, perhaps with pain, what he is renouncing when he does not marry, only the one who knows that he can be happy and find fulfilment in marriage, is also able to renounce it in the true Christian sense. But although the word 'renounce' can have a good and correct meaning, it does not properly fit the situation.

In the first place: the celibacy of Jesus was not due to a 'renunciation', that is, a lessening of love, but to an unheard of fullness of a love which would not be restricted to one partner and limited to one's own family. Instead it is able, and willing, to be a partner to many and to regard many as its family, just as Jesus could say, pointing to his disciples, 'These are my mother and my brothers' (Mt 1:50). In a special way the voluntary celibate, like Jesus, seeks for solidarity with those unmarried for whom celibacy = aloneness 'is actually no virtue but their fate in life. Celibacy is drawn to those who are shut up in a lack of expectation and a feeling of resignation' (J.B. Metz) — those who in our modern society are alone and isolated, withoutt any human partner.

The celibate performs a special service for marriage itself. When undertaken for the sake of the kingdom of God, celibacy becomes a definite sign that marriage, the highest value in creation (certainly according to Gen 1:27 the union of man and wife is the goal of all creation), belongs to the sphere of the 'penultimate', and that it can only come to its complete intrinsic fulfilment if the two partners make them themselves free for the ultimate great reality — the coming kingdom of God. Celibacy does this because it runs counter to the absolutising of marriage (and also to the idolisation and overvaluation of sexuality, which have been a threat to mankind throughout human history) and shows that marriage is a value which is relative — in the best sense.[15] In this way celibacy indicates how marriage can be lived in a way which will give true happiness, in that freedom which grows out of faith in the coming Kingdom of God. For it is only in the hope that all alienation will be done away with in God's kingdom, only in the belief and expectation that there all that is ineffective and limited will come to fulfilment, it is only then that the impossibility of complete fulfilment, which in spite of all love every marriage experiences, will be overcome. But until then, the voluntary celibate can show to the married that it is possible to live in the freedom of the dawning kingdom, 'that interhuman relationship even at a distance can be endured, and that once again the highest personality, grace, God himself, is present in this impersonality and incomplete fulfilment. To devote oneself unreservedly to others, to bring men together when they are hopelessly estranged, to show personality where there is alienation, that is what the celibate life means. Surely this is Christian! Only a sophist can assert that celibacy is due to the influence of paganism' (E. Klinger).

Not only has celibacy significance for marriage: marriage also has significance for celibacy. As W. Kasper points out, 'just as the one who for Christ's sake is unmarried reveals his freedom to the married, so also the eschatological character of marriage shows in return that an eschatological form of life need not mean a flight from the world but is instead a particular mode of service for the world and for others. The two modes of Christian life must therefore be understood in their reciprocal relationship. They both stand and fall together. Vocations to celibacy are a sign of sound Christian marriages: the devaluation of celibacy necessarily leads also to a failure to recognise the Christian values of marriage.'

In a very personal way, T. Salomon, a member of 'Marriage

Encounter', has expressed the connection between celibacy and marriage
as follows: "I am convinced that the one is impossible without the other;
they both necessarily belong together. The sacrament of marriage can
only be lived permanently when there is someone there who constantly
reminds both partners of their vocation, which is to be sign of God's
love. Who can do this better than the one who says, "I wish to devote
myself and live entirely, not only for a single individual, but for all of
you, for a (quite concrete) community"? Just as the husband and wife
while administering the sacrament in the presence of the community
testify to their determination to give their partner priority in their life,
and by their efforts in maintaining their unity and love to make God
sacramentally visible to others, similarly the priest, by his determination
to seek to be available for many, to live in relationship to them, with
a quite deliberate renunciation of a union with a single partner, points
out that all our human search for union and relationship of love has
its origin and fulfilment in God. That is the meaning of celibacy for
the sake of the kingdom of heaven. The priest will, can, must, derive
the strength to persevere in this manner of life essentially from the
community, which shows him that it is entirely reasonable to devote
himself for love, shows him an example and joins in supporting him.'

When one considers the relationship between marriage and celibacy,
it is surely no accident that the present crisis of voluntary celibacy for
the sake of the kingdom of God corresponds to a deep crisis of marriage,
and vice versa. This is one more reason why the Church must devote
more effort not only to the pastoral care of marriage, but also to an
express campaign for evangelical celibacy.

But celibacy for the sake of God's kingdom does not aim merely
at a greater extension of love: it is not only the sign of freedom
for the married: on the contrary — and here we come to the kernel
of the matter — it can become what is perhaps the most impressive
witness to the coming of the kingdom. Paul Claudel remarks in
his *Satin Slipper* (from the man's point of view) that 'woman
is a promise which will not be kept'. In other words: in the mutual
love of two human beings, the promise of ultimate life-fulfilment
beckons. Yet, this promise will be disappointed, must be
disappointed. Human love is certainly great, the greatest in the
world. But even in its highest form it is only a prevision and first
instalment, a hopeful sign therefore of its own ultimate fulfilment
which God alone can give. This does not mean that married love
is in competition with the love of God, and intended perhaps as
a means to that love. There is only one Love — God himself.

THE EVANGELICAL COUNSELS 125

Marriage has a share of it — but the part is not the whole.

Certainly, neither does the one who has chosen celibacy achieve the fulness of love: but in his 'unnormal' mode of life he maintains in visible symbol the stimulus that one may venture to build on a promise that will be kept, that is, the promise of the kingdom in which all human yearning for love is satisfied. Certainly the one who is married can and should also live in this attitude of love and faith. In view of the coming kingdom, he can and should live 'as though he were not married' (cf. 1 Cor 7:29), i.e., so that for him marriage is not the ultimate good but is opening itself for the coming Lord. To this extent there must be an element of celibacy included in every Christian marriage — the surrender of marriage and of the spouse for one's greater fulfilment. Nevertheless, this absolute concentration on the kingdom takes visible form in those who choose celibacy: it is not concealed in the interior of the life of faith, nor is it a merely verbal profession; it is a truly living reality, especially in the physical, sensitive and emotional spheres. The structures of this world, to which marrying and being married really belong (not merely as *one* value among others, but as the supreme value which includes all created values) are as it were broken open by the celibate, because he relies on an absolute promise and lives by it.

The metaphor which K. Rahner has used to illustrate all the evangelical counsels is therefore particularly appropriate to celibacy: there is a saying that a bird in the hand is worth two in the bush. One who according to the Gospel lives without marrying is proclaiming 'No, I prefer the two', that is, prefer the coming kingdom of God. For '"the two in the bush" are really believed in only when one releases the "one in the hand", and in fact before it is taken from one, and before the "two in the bush" are caught.' Rahner goes on to comment: 'This hopeful faith, this seizing upon God's future, can be really accomplished and prove its existence only by the surrender of this-world values. It is not as if these values were in direct opposition to faith, hope and charity, and cannot be positively integrated into the existence of these virtues. But the values of this world, and particularly marriage, the highest of them can be enjoyed without hopeful faith in the kingdom of God. Consequently, this faith can give serious proof and visible testimony of itself only when values are relinquished 'whose positive and direct renunciation is, in general, not sensible and justified except when one is reaching out for grace', for the dawning kingdom. Thus, the relinquishing of values such as marriage becomes a concrete act of faith. It is 'in itself an expression and manifestation of faith which in reaching out for the grace of God separates itself from simple absorption in the world' and allows the hope for the approaching kingdom to shine forth.

If one considers the whole meaning of an evangelical celibacy, and if one values celibacy above all as an eschatological sign, its connection with the official priesthood will be seen to be much closer than is expressed in the clichés of recent controversies, especially the facile phrase 'the Church's rigid celibacy law'. Priestly celibacy means: to surrender oneself in the centre of one's existence to the task officially 'representing' Christ. Consequently the priest must proclaim, with the greatest personal emphasis, the central point of the official activity which he must undertake: that the kingdom of God is already coming and 'the structure of this world is passing away'(1 Cor 7:31). The summons spoken at ordination, *Imitamini quod tractatis* (Do in your own life what you are officially accomplishing) can become especially concrete in celibacy. The life of the priest should be the confirmation of what he continually preaches and celebrates sacramentally — the death and Resurrection of Christ, the hope of his coming in glory, the life eternal in which 'there is no more marrying' (Mk 12:25). What alternatives are there? In what other way can testimony be given of God's approaching world? By means of the comfortable parochial houses in countries of the West? Or through the middleclass lifestyle which most priests nowadays accept? Or through public influence and association with worldly power, still defended by the Church in many places? Does the credibility of the official teaching not require some proof that costs the official teacher something and shows that the preacher is the first to listen to his own words?

Frequently such questions are met by the objection that celibacy no longer witnesses to anything. A sign loses its effectiveness when it is no longer understood: and, it is argued, this is precisely the case with celibacy today: even 'good Catholics' do not any longer see it as a sign. One must answer: according to Catholic theology an essential part of a sacramental sign is the 'form' — the words which interpret the meaning of the sign. If, then, it is really true that parish communities no longer understand the significance of celibacy, that poses a serious question for the preacher and teacher of religion: In what way and how often is this sign explained? Enquiries about this have revealed apparent deficiencies which are often startling. It is no wonder that so few priestly vocations are stimulated!

But celibacy is not only an 'eschatological sign'; it is also a continual 'thorn in the flesh' (2 Cor 12:7) of the priest. All his life long, celibacy poses the question: Is the law, according to which he started to devote himself to the priestly ministry, still of value? Is the kingdom of God really the 'one pearl' and the 'treasure in the field' for which everything else is to be sacrificed? Life without marriage is very demanding in real terms, and it is a standard by which a young man can measure the seriousness of his offering to devote his life to the service of Christ. It remains such a standard through his entire life.

Last, but not least, the celibacy of the priest sets him free for the undivided service to Christ's cause. The father of the house of God's family, the shepherd of his flock, should also be entirely available for them: he should give to his love that breadth which Jesus has indicated when promising his disciples 'new' brothers and sisters, mothers and children (Mk 10:30). In this sense Pope John Paul II in a letter to priests said emphatically that celibacy is not only an eschatological sign, 'but has also great social importance for the ministries for the people of God in the present life. Through his celibacy the priest becomes a "man for others", not in the same way as a man who unites himself with a woman in a community of marriage thus becoming, particularly in his own family, "a man for others" — for his wife and with her for the children to whom they give the gift of life. While the priest renounces the fatherhood proper to the married, he gains another fatherhood, indeed almost another motherhood, when he reflects upon what the Apostle St Paul says about the children for whom he is suffering the pangs of giving birth. They are the children of his spirit, whom the good Shepherd has entrusted to his care. They are numerous, more numerous than a normal human family can be.'

It is true that the requirement of celibacy as a condition for ordination could be withdrawn. The absolute linking of celibacy and ordination is — as everyone knows — a matter of church law,[16] Western Church law, to be more precise. But instead of the debates about celibacy which are so popular today and yet so utterly fruitless, should one not start with the actual situation, which will obtain at least for the time being, where the two are linked together: and should one not consider the inner significance and opportunity which this linking contains? Pope John Paul II called celibacy 'a gift of grace from the Spirit'. The Catholic Church of the West, in setting celibacy as a precondition for ordination, is proclaiming with the utmost clarity that for its office-bearers it wishes to have only 'charismatics', that is, men who have received particular gifts of grace from the Holy Spirit, and are striving for more. In this it shows its concern for the essential unity of spiritual office and spiritual mode of life, a unity already attested in Scripture.[17] Celibacy is a sign which declares that the man who is to 'represent' Christ officially, and like him is to guarantee the approach of the kingdom, is putting the sign into practice in his own life. And if it is true that the witness of celibacy for the sake of God's kingdom belongs essentially to the Church (which as a whole must live according to the Gospel), it would certainly be undesirable if this witness were only or mostly to be found in those lay people who follow the evangelical counsels, and not among those who represent the Church officially.

It is often objected that celibacy and church office are two different vocations, and that consequently celibacy should be left to the free choice of the individual so as to solve the problem of the shortage of priests. But, whatever may be said in individual cases, the objection often overlooks essential elements of the question.

(1) This objection is often based on a mistaken and onesided idea of charisma and freedom. On this point I agree entirely with J. Kremer. The church law of celibacy is accused of contradicting 1 Cor 7:7 (in which St Paul describes celibacy as a charisma). The objection regards charisma as a kind of pre-existing inborn aptitude for celibacy. But this is not the Apostle's concept of charisma. 'By this word he means ministries and gifts which the Holy Spirit produces in the community, and to which the individual can open or close himself. . . . Paul can therefore warn the community at Corinth "But be zealous for the greater charismata", that is, give ever more room to the Holy Spirit in your midst and in your life. The demand for celibacy as a precondition for

ordination assumes that the candidate has or will be granted this charisma, and that the Spirit of God (and not a natural predisposition as such) will enable him to live without marriage for the sake of God's kingdom. The institutional regulation does not take away the nature of celibacy as a grace. It serves instead to produce an environment which makes it possible or easier for many to be taken up by the Spirit of God for a witness of this kind in the service of Christ' (J. Kremer).

It should not be overlooked that, in general, human freedom of choice is not opposed to an institutional and social environment but presupposes it. It is a caricature of freedom to say that free choice takes place only in the isolation of the individual, relying on himself alone, and that freedom is exercised only when there are no preconditions. On the contrary, a free decision has always social presuppositions as well, and probably much more than we realise. Modern depth psychology and sociological analysis of society should make us alert to this. A free decision always means the free acceptance or refusal of an existing situation. It involves a mixture of motives and impulses which come to us from our situation in society and in history (resulting from education, language, social values and fashions).

To return to the concrete question of celibacy: the Church could certainly change the law which requires celibacy in the priest, and leave to each one the choice of his own lifestyle. Yet even then this free decision would not be without presuppositions. The precondition set by church order would no longer be present; but there would still be the whole influence of present-day social pressures towards marriage, pervasive pansexuality, the difficulties (especially: isolation, loss of community and security) which derive from the 'homelessness' of the unmarried in the present social context, etc.[18] Consequently the retention today of the law of celibacy can also be seen as a barrier against the social conditioning which today operates in a completely different direction. But above all, the institutional link between the charisma of celibacy and vocation to the priesthood need not imply any limitation of freedom but a truly biblical demand to 'strive' for this charisma.

It is often argued or implied that if there were no obligation of celibacy the Church would have sufficient vocations for the priesthood. This is debatable at least as far as young people are concerned. Certainly, a whole series of male lay theologians say that they would be ready to accept priestly ordination if this obligation did not apply. Nevertheless, it is doubtful if this interpretation applies in general (and not merely to a few). Undoubtedly, many lay theologians articulate their prejudices against the official Church by attacking celibacy. It may be asked, however, if these prejudices would not take another form if this requirement were to be abolished. Consequently, the observation of E. Schillebeeckx seems to be much more to the point: he says that celibacy is for many a prominent feature of the official Church, and that their rejection of celibacy is a symptom of the inability of many to identify with the official Church.[19]

It is occasionally said that one can be in favour of voluntary celibacy in the spirit of the Gospel, but not of linking it with church office. This could be merely a verbal assertion if the person who makes it does not devote himself with all his power (and if possible by his own lifestyle) to the cause of celibacy in the Church, thus producing an environment in which the vocation to celibacy can develop. Here I agree entirely with G. Lohfink: 'Before the link between leadership of the community and celibacy can be broken . . . the laity in church ministry must be penetrated by a lively spirituality guided by the Gospel — a lively spirituality that not only values the charisma of celibacy, but also frequently produces it in individual cases. Only in this way can justifiable anxieties and worries be eventually removed, and the way cleared for the lifting of the law of celibacy.' Lohfink himself holds that such a lifting of the law is desirable, 'but certainly only on condition that the environment favourable to the charisma of voluntary celibacy should continue to develop everywhere in the Church — a positive attitude, live visible communities, a live spirituality guided by the Gospel. For this reason I hold it to be wrong, and indeed harmful, to advocate only the abolition of celibacy unless at the same time one strives just as expressly and urgently for the cultivation of this charisma and for a deeper spirituality. A call only for abolition will in fact produce an effect quite opposed to the real objective. It will increase in many Catholics the mistrust which it is supposed to diminish: indeed it will actually evoke anxiety about a new breed of ecclesiastical officials who are just officials and functionaries, who no longer devote themselves and their whole life to service of the Gospel.' For Lohfink therefore, the condition for lifting the celibacy law is this: 'Only when a sufficient number of teachers of religion, parish assistants, priests, theology professors and bishops live according to the model of Jesus, only then can the warning sign implied in the celibacy obligation be dropped. It would be simply unnecessary'.

The truth of the last sentence need not be gone into here. The point is that, despite all the convergence of priestly office and celibacy, the ancient and venerable link between them, institutionalised in canon law, could be broken under certain conditions. But the unity of official mission and actual lifestyle, which celibacy concretely expresses and produces, must not be broken without providing a substitute. If, therefore, someone has good reason for his certainty that in the future there should also be a married priesthood, he must propose a model in which the unity of office and lifestyle can be effected in a different but analogous manner.

Such a model could be a *vir probatus* — the ordination of a man who by his previous practice of a mature Christian life has shown and continues to show that his official activity is actually guaranteed by a life spent in the following of Christ. In him the unity of office and lifestyle is 'verified' by his record; in a young man by his readiness for (and incipient practice of) a life of special following of Christ, a life which includes celibacy. This could be a model for the association of a celibate with a married priesthood. Certainly, one should not be too quick to assume that such an arrangement would solve all difficulties. Nevertheless, the *vir probatus* seems so far to provide the only useful model for a married priesthood. If it is put into practice, it could be, as H. Urs v. Balthasar says, that 'in the Church of the future unmarried priests would be in the minority. It could be. But it could also be that the example of the ministry would light up the evident rightness and indispensability of this form of life in the Church. It could be that we must pass through a period of hunger and thirst, but that this deprivation will awaken new vocations, or, more correctly, the courage to answer the vocations which are never wanting . . .'.

The present-day debate about celibacy gives the impression that the crisis of priestly celibacy is due to its being connected by law with ordination. This is probably not true. The real crisis is due to the way in which a celibate life is lived. It was unfortunate in the past, and still is, that celibacy has in fact been separated from its whole spiritual context, that is, from the obligation to demonstrate personal sympathy in one's life and official action. It has thus become a kind of exclusive shibboleth. Instead of devoting the whole of life to the following of the Lord, one 'observes' celibacy. But can that be done?

St Thomas Aquinas regards the three evangelical counsels as forming an indivisible unity: they are like three sides of a single prism — that is, of one life which is set free for God according to the example of the Gospel. Celibacy is therefore only *one* side of an indivisible whole. Is it then surprising if its practice as an isolated fragment cannot be convincing? Where a man does not devote himself to the whole call of the Gospel to follow Christ, his celibacy is like a foreign body in his life plan. Since, then, the

Church for adequate reasons demands from the priest celibacy for the sake of God's kingdom, and that he should in this point live 'according to the Gospel', this is not possible without somehow putting the other counsels into practice. If this is not done, celibacy cannot be a convincing sign or be lived in that joy which is the mark of Christ's disciples. Instead, it will be only a burden and consequently a matter of continual personal and ecclesial 'reconsideration'.

E. Schillebeeckx rightly says that 'the continual appeal to the Law is in the view of many all the less credible because insistence on this law is not accompanied by a real evangelical availability in poverty, renunciation of power and titles of honour, and devotion to one's fellows... What significance has celibacy in a Church in which one strives for honour, wealth and a comfortable middle-class life? To be sure, the official Church does not approve these things, but they are tolerated in a broadminded spirit and do not lead to mandatory deprival of office.'

On the other hand, when celibacy is integrated in a life of following Christ, it is even today a convincing and respected sign. I have, for example, never heard that anyone has found the celibacy of Mother Teresa (can anyone imagine her as a married woman?) to be a problem, or the celibacy of the Brothers of Taizé. Here one can feel that celibacy has a harmonious place in the whole of their lives. For the priest also, it must be an important objective that his celibacy fits harmoniously into the whole of his life. But his effort cannot be successful except when he practises the other two forms of the imitation of Christ — obedience and poverty. This is required of the priest, at least to some degree: at his ordination he promises obedience to his bishop and Canon Law expects from him a certain sobriety in his lifestyle. Yet in contrast to the definite obligation of celibacy, these requirements often do not lead to any practical consequences. It is, therefore, appropriate at this point to direct our attention to obedience and poverty.

b) *Obedience* Jesus was the obedient one *par excellence*. In the christological hymn of the epistle to the Philippians (2:5-11), St Paul calls out to the community: 'Have the same mind in you as Christ Jesus, who ... was obedient unto ... the death on the cross'. This obedience he understands and explains as a radical emptying of himself: Jesus keeps back nothing for himself, holds on to nothing, but humbles and surrenders himself completely. That is the fundamental shape of biblical obedience.

Obedience of this kind is essentially determined by listening. That person is obedient who does not concentrate on himself but instead is attentive to the demand of the hour, in which he discerns the will of God. He is then available and ready to do what he perceives to be God's will. Thus, an obedient person regards his whole existence as a surrender, i.e., a going out of himself when called. Another central text of the New Testament expresses the same idea in the following way: 'Christ speaks at his entrance into the world: Sacrifice and oblation you did not desire, but a body you prepared for me; holocausts and sin-offerings were not pleasing to you. Then I said, Behold I have come, as it is written of me in the book, to do your will, O God' (Heb 10:5f). Thus Christ understood his whole existence (his body which is prepared for him) as something which will be given up to do the will of God. 'My meat is to do the will of him who sent me and to finish his work' (Jn 4:34). 'My meat' — what touches the innermost basis of existence, from which one lives — consists in putting myself at the disposal of God and his work.

These broad outlines — obedience as a sacrifice of freedom, as a giving up when called upon, as a radical availability — are the decisive structural elements of biblical obedience. Independence, freedom and personal decision are a great possession, indeed the greatest possession of mankind. The sinner thinks that it is the supreme use of freedom when a man does what pleases him on every particular occasion, when he uses his freedom for himself, for his own pleasure, for whatever he wishes. But it is not so: freedom is at its greatest when it is exercised and voluntarily surrendered at God's call, a call which ever meets us afresh in the here and now.

Obedience of this kind is required of all Christians. St Paul's call is to everyone: 'Have the same mind in you as Christ Jesus' (Phil 2:5). Nevertheless, Jesus expects a more radical, a more clearly significant form of this obedience from those to whom he gives a special commision of service for the kingdom. Thus, at the sending out of the disciples (Lk 9:57ff; 10:1ff), to the requirement of poverty is added the injunction to have that radical availability which keeps only one thing in mind — the service of the kingdom. The same attitude is clear in the life of St Paul: listening to each particular situation he becomes 'all things to all men' (1 Cor 9:22) in order to win them for the kingdom of God.

Only he who is able to hear and be sensitive to the manifold call of reality has also the openness to let himself be touched by the needs, the anxieties and concerns of his brothers. Only he who can surrender himself, that is, who can listen and go out from himself and give himself, is also able to let himself be worn out by the justified and sometimes not so justified wishes and expectations of those around him. One who is available through obedience is able to put aside his own wishes, prejudices and favourite interests, for the sake of others. He can work together with them, he is able to accept criticism and is ready for what comes. Thus obedience is a prerequisite for being a 'man for others' in a special way. But it is just this which is an essential part of priestly ministry in imitation of the obedient Lord.

It is, however, not only because the official Church must be guided by the basic attitudes of Jesus that priesthood involves obedience. The most important reason of all is that the bearer of church office has the obligation to pass on something which he does not possess of himself but which he himself obeys and must pass on to others. Consquently, a priest who does not first listen before he delivers the message is fundamentally a counterfeiter who is not circulating genuine currency and real values but instead is carrying out a deception with sham metal of his own making. Priestly office, therefore, is either founded on personal listening to the word of God or else degenerates into a 'popedom' which merely discharges functions. How can a person prepare a community for the kingdom of God, and proclaim the word of God to it, if he has not first listened to it himself? If someone seeks his advice, how can one say with authority 'Do this, or that!' if he has not first listened to God in prayer and asked him what is his will for this man.

Besides this readiness to listen, the candidate for ordination, at the ordination itself, makes a public and binding surrender of his freedom in carrying out the pastoral work of the Church, a work for which the bishop (and the major superior in a religious order) bears the ultimate responsibility. This promise of obedience is the concrete answer of those whom God and the Church have called to the official mission. Strictly speaking the promise of obedience is made, not to the bishop, but to God, who draws and encourages the candidate to this offering of his freedom, and to the community, which needs the availability of the priest. Looked at in this way, ordination implies an obligation to offer oneself for the official mission of the Church. But this sacrifice is a real *offering*, a giving up of self, a renunciation of some degree of 'self' fulfilment. Occasionally one may hear priests say, 'I will not put up with being pushed around by the bishop, by the diocesan chancery, by the parish priest, by the parishioners!' They are, it may be, in difficult situations, or have been given assignments or instructions which do not appeal to them. In such cases, one must ask if this is not precisely the result of the offering of their lives which they promised at their ordination. St Paul has compared his apostolic ministry to the sacrifice in the Temple: 'Even if I am being poured out as a drink-offering upon the sacrificial service of your faith, I rejoice in it and share my joy with you' (Phil 2:17). Paul therefore regards his life as a holocaust for the Church. Similarly, at ordination the priest promises that in the final analysis he will permit himself to be 'pushed around', that he will be a living sacrifice with Christ and will allow himself to be caught up into Christ's obedience unto death. Obedience is, therefore, ultimately an offering of one's life 'unto the death of the cross'. It cannot be fulfilled more cheaply.

In the daily spiritual exercises of the priest, obedience could take concrete form in this 'examination of conscience':

(1) Can I listen? Do I take the trouble to come out from my own circle and be open for the call of God and my neighbour? This listening takes place first of all in prayer, seeking to find God's will for my own life, for the community entrusted to me, and for those who seek my counsel. Secondly, I must 'listen' to the situation, to 'the signs of the times', to the call of the hour. Neither in prayer nor in daily life is the call easy to recognise or to plan in advance, just as the Samaritan had not provided for the man fallen among robbers while planning his journey. Only the one who listens will hear the call. Can I, therefore, listen?

(2) When I have listened, am I available? That is, can I give up my previous plans, my wishes and pet ideas, in order to attend

to what I heard and to take appropriate action? Am I there entirely for the community (the parish)? Do I have time for them?[20] Do I allow myself to be worn out by their wishes and expectations? Am I prepared to put aside my own form of devotion and my own attitudes, for the sake of the community? What is the concrete meaning of 'becoming all things to all men' in a parish where the Legion is to be found as well as the Left intelligentsia, the young who flirt with agnosticism and scepticism, as well as the Schönstatt Society, the Focolare Movement and other groups? Am I a kind of hierarch, a Very Reverend, a Pasha for my parishioners, or do I try to live my life for others? Do I look beyond my parish to the whole Church and its world mission, to political events, to Third World problems, to 'alternative' movements: and do I seek to recognise here a challenging call and answer it appropriately?

(3) Can I withdraw into the background in order to work *with* others? Can I take advice or criticism from the laity? Do I make it easy for others to express a criticism or am I so dismissive that no one even ventures to criticise me to my face?

These test questions, which a priest must forever be asking himself, can be the concrete form of the 'self-emptying' and 'obedience unto death on the cross' of the hymn in the epistle to the Philippians.

c) *Poverty*   St Paul speaks of Christ as the one who, though he was rich, became poor for our sake, so that through his poverty we may become rich (cf. 2 Cor 8:9). The poverty of Jesus took different forms — the poverty of the crib in Bethlehem, his modest lifestyle in Nazareth, the poverty of his public life. All the Gospels tell us that in his public life Jesus led a life of poverty and need. 'The foxes have holes, the birds of the air have nests, but the Son of Man has nowhere to lay his head' (Lk 9:28). Jesus made himself dependent on the alms which the people, and particularly rich women, gave to him. Finally, his life culminated in the radical poverty of the cross.

Wherever people came into contact with Jesus, they were called to share in his poverty. Here we must recall his many warnings about the dangers of riches and possessions, and his insistence on the value of poverty. 'Blessed are the poor . . . but woe to you who are rich, for you are (now) receiving your comfort in full. Woe to you who are well fèd, for you shall be hungry' (Lk 6:20, 24f). The kingdom of God is promised to those who do not live in the desire of possessions and influence, who do not base their lives on their wealth, their efficiency and their power, but are empty, open and available for God and his call. The faith which Jesus demands is the faith of Abraham who, relying on God's promise, left everything — his home, his family, even his only son. To attain the kingdom of God a man must part with all other pearls in order to buy this one: he must do everything to acquire the treasure in the field (Mk 13:44f); a man who has rich possessions is in the extreme danger of neglecting the call of God's kingdom and of going along the broad way which leads to destruction (Mt 7:13). 'How hard will it be for the wealthy to enter the kingdom of God!' (Mk 10:23). The rich man is in danger of seeking his own security and living on his capital, as we hear in Lk 12:18f.: 'Now you have many good things laid up, to last for many years; take your ease, eat, drink and be merry'. But the hands of the poor man are empty: he expects everything from God in the approaching kingdom.

Poverty (and wealth) are to be understood here as a real lack (or abundance) of possessions, and not simply a mental attitude, like a spiritual indifference or frugality. Yet the additional words in St Matthew (5:3), 'Blessed are the poor *in spirit*', indicate that a merely external lack of possessions is not sufficient for the poverty intended by the Gospel. External poverty must be accompanied by a corresponding interior poverty, a spiritual readiness to do without, and to be available — the will to base one's life not on oneself, but on God's promise.

By this call to poverty the Gospel does not in any way condemn wealth completely. Property and the use of material things are indeed, from Creation onwards, positively good. Ownership is the expression of the freedom and independence of mankind and its controlling position in the world. Besides, even in voluntary poverty it is not possible for anyone to renounce all possession and every use of earthly goods. Even the poorest has a minimum of property and a possibility of disposing of it. Fundamentally possession and property are positively good. But the world and its values are no longer as they were originally planned by God. Through human sin they have, as it were, lost their innocence. Mankind should have thankfully accepted the things of the world, used them sensibly, looking towards God and the purpose of life, with gratitude to God: possession and wealth should have remained, as it were, transparent, thus making it possible to see God through them. Instead of this, the sinner makes material things into false gods, setting them up as absolute values. But this makes him unfree for the greater good: created things block him from seeing what really matters. The sinner defines himself by the possession of material goods, instead of using them as a means to achieve the greater good of love.

Christ, therefore, by his choice of poverty, his renunciation of wealth and possessions, tears apart the narcotic net of the desire for wealth, the search for self-satisfaction, the craving for worldly things. He sets up a new pattern of liberated life, which refuses to become a slave to worldly things and is free for God and his service.

For this reason a certain degree of distance from possessions is required from all believers. Since it is difficult for the rich — indeed, as Jesus says, it is humanly impossible — to attain salvation, since poverty is shown to be the mode of life which corresponds to the promise of God's kingdom, the spirit of poverty is fundamentally bound up with the Christian faith. This is true for all Christians without exception. The Beatitude and the warning about the rich is spoken to all. This was demonstrated in the first Christian communities, in which membership already implied some form of surrendering possessions (cf. Acts 2:44f; 4:34f.). Moreover, the saying of St Paul that Christians should possess things as if they did not own them (cf. 1 Cor 7:29f.), his demand that they should have an attitude of detachment from possessions, is addressed to all. But within the poverty recommended to all and the warning about riches issued to all, these are different forms of particular vocations and different ways of carrying them out.

One of these vocations to poverty is found in the specific lifestyle of the Apostle or disciple of Jesus. In the instructions given to the disciples before they set out on their mission, the particular form and function of this poverty is described. They were to take nothing with them on their journey, no bag, no purse, no money, no shoes, no bread, no spare tunic (Lk 9:1f; 10:1ff). They were to be satisfied with what was put before them and offered to them: they should not demand anything. There is a triple motive for this poverty of the disciples:

(1) The credibility of the proclamation of God's kingdom is at stake. In the preacher who is poor, needy, unpretentious, the claim of the message itself can appear unadulterated and without distortion. This is frequently pointed out in the Pauline writings also. In Philippians (1:17) St Paul says that many who are preaching Christ are motivated by self-interest. Although such preaching is not without value, it runs contrary to sincerity and grieves the Apostle. On the contrary, Paul's glory is to have accepted nothing from anyone, although — as he says expressly in 1 Cor 9:4ff — he would had a just claim to be maintained by the community. 'Nevertheless, we did not make use of this right, but we endure all things [i.e., earn our keep], so as not to cause any hindrance to the Gospel of Christ' (9:12). 'Because I was not dependent on anyone, I made myself a slave to all, in order to win as many as possible' (9:19). The first epistle of Peter makes a similar call to the presbyters not to shepherd the flock entrusted to them with a view to sordid gain. The poverty of the preacher helps the unhindered exposition of the Gospel, and his own credibility.

(2) In the poverty of the disciple and the Apostle, the content of their message comes visibly to the hearers. Their poverty is like a 'sacrament' which makes it possible to see the Gospel and the one who has been influenced by it. Not with words alone, but through his life, the Apostle must proclaim the central point of the 'glad news', that the kingdom of God is approaching and the structure of this world is passing away, that the crucified Lord is the risen Lord, that death means life and true life cannot be won without dying. He must himself incorporate his message. The cross of Christ and the hope of resurrection appear in the hopeful desire of the Apostles 'to be crucified with Christ': and they get their wish: they 'are to this present hour poorly clothed (and) toil and work with their own hands' (1 Cor 4:11ff). The message of cross and resurrection become visible in the poverty of the Apostle. In this way, the preacher becomes the living sign of his message, a sign that the form of this world is passing away and that the Lord is coming to set us free.

(3) A third motive for a lifestyle of poverty can be found in the New Testament. The poverty demanded in the Gospel, as the incident of the rich young man particularly shows (Mk 10:17ff), is a prerequisite for the following of Jesus, and simultaneously

a matter of giving one's wealth to the poor in order to follow him. Just as the poverty of Jesus was the form of his love for mankind — 'he became poor to make us rich' (2 Cor 8:9) — so also the poverty of the disciples is a means of exercising love for men, and particularly for the poor, who are the brothers and sisters of Jesus. Poverty leads to solidarity with the poor, to greater availability in love. Only one who is himself poor can really be a friend of the poor, the insignificant, the outsider. J.B. Metz remarks: 'Poverty as a protest against the dictatorship of ownership and possession, of downright self-assertion . . . drives one into actual solidarity with those of the poor for whom poverty is not a virtue but their situation in life, and an unreasonable social imposition'.

For all these reasons it is very appropriate that the priest who is to deliver the message of the coming kingdom and to proclaim the death and Resurrection of Christ, should himself lead the way in practising the first of all the beatitudes. This he should do in two ways: (1) by a style of life which, if not actually poor, is at least simple, and (2) by a special love for the poor and a feeling of solidarity with them. He must ask, as a serious question for himself and the community he leads, whether the poor are the 'preferred ones' as they were for Jesus. Or are the preferred ones the rich, the solid middle class, who in general have more to contribute, who know 'how to behave themselves', and with whom one 'can afford to be seen'? Who is the particular object of our interest and love? Clearly the very Gospel is at stake insofar as the rich, the middle class, the well-to-do and the 'responsible' are given preference, as happens often in the Church of the West. 'If a man comes into your assembly with a golden ring and dressed in fine clothes, and if at the same time there comes a poor man dressed in dirty clothes, and you pay special attention to the one who is wearing fine clothes and say "Sit down here in a good place", and you say to the poor man "You stand over here" or, "sit down by my footstool', are you not making distinctions among yourselves, and becoming judges with evil motives? Listen, my beloved brothers, did not God choose the poor of the world to be rich in faith and heirs of the kingdom which he promised to those who love him? But you dishonoured the poor man . . .' (Jas 2:2ff). It is the attitude to the poor, the insignificant and the outsiders which determines whether Gospel poverty is an empty phrase or a living reality.

Furthermore: what is our reaction to world poverty, how do we treat the 'Lazarus at the door'? Today, Lazarus is everywhere. Television brings him not only to our door but right into our comfortable livingroom. Does he receive only the fragments which fall from the table, or does he receive more? We must realise the plain fact that today's consumer society is essentially shaped by artificially created needs which are then satisfied by the myriad products of our affluent society. It is therefore often very difficult to decide in a particular case what is a real necessity and therefore justifies production. Something necessary for life, or appropriate for a modest lifestyle, will not give rise to any special difficulty. But what about the numerous artificial needs and comforts of the society today? How far can an individual, or a community which wishes to respond to the call for evangelical poverty, cooperate in this? There will be many borderline cases and grey areas.

A reflection, which as far as I know derives from Heinrich Spaemann, can serve as a help to making a decision. If one has to decide about some questionable purchase, or some building scheme (parochial house, church . . .), or some expensive holiday, etc.), he should double the price being considered, and ask himself if he would be ready to pay this increased price. If the answer is yes, let him proceed in the following manner: pay the amount demanded and assign the remaining half to the needs of the poor. Such a procedure has a psychological impact: it means the poor are always a factor in my decisions about property, comforts and advantages, and are always by my side. And there are real results: I give to another a share in everything I possess and procure for myself or which gives me pleasure: I tax myself for the benefit of the poor and make myself equal to them — even in small things — in order to practise the love for the poor which the Gospel demands. A practice of this kind could be very important for one's own day-to-day decisions or those of a community or parish.

To have regard to poverty in the world is especially appropriate to-day. F. Wulf rightly remarks: "If charismatic poverty wishes to be a contemporary answer to the call of the Gospel, it must, it seems, look for solidarity with the exploited, the helpless and especially with those who are the victims of the way our society is structured. Solidarity of this kind, if it is to be more than a pious wish, means sharing in the life and fate of the others . . . . It will urge me to better the lot of the poor, to bring about an improvement in their situation, to stand up for right and justice.'

But poverty is more than a problem of the structures of society. The priest, who has been entrusted with the word of God as a 'Gospel for the poor', must also ask himself questions about his personal lifestyle. Does he live in a way which befits his official activity and is not an obstacle to his preaching? Can, for example, the poorest man in the parish feel at home in the priest's presence, or when he comes to him does he find in the priest's house and dress and conduct a different sociological world? To what extent does the priest himself feel something of the insecurity which the following of Jesus involves, as we read in the Gospel? Or, is the motto to be allround security and insurance? When does he renounce something which he could quite properly have, in order that Paul's words about Jesus could also apply to him: 'He was rich, yet for our sake he became poor, that through his poverty we might become rich' (2 Cor 8:9)?

d) *Summary*   Celibacy, obedience and poverty are a concrete form of a life lived in following Jesus. This form is imposed on the priest in particular, in order to achieve the unity of his mission and life, of his office and actual lifestyle. 'Put your life under the mystery of the cross': words spoken to the candidate at ordination.

Is his life lived under this mystery? Has he the courage to pass on the 'disconcerting' message of the cross by word and by the example of his life? 'The more disconcerting the Christian message which we preach, the more helpful will our preaching be, the more up-to-date and more committed to the world. Have we the courage to make our message uncomfortable in our life and preaching? Not only by preaching about involvement in the world but also about flight from the world? Not only by preaching about marriage but also by telling people about the "folly" of celibacy? Not only by pointing out to the lawfulness of riches but also by preaching evangelical poverty? Not only by speaking about personal self-fulfilment, but also by preaching about obedience? Do we venture to speak about the explosive force of the cross, using so-called "empty words" such as "sacrifice", "representation", "atonement"? and to make some of these words visible in our precarious "homelessness" without wife and children, in our obedient "openness to being transferred", and in our acceptance of the cross thus imposed on us?' (H. Schurmann).

For Paul, the life of the community essentially depended on the way in which he practised the mystery of the cross in his own life. After saying 'we always carry about in our body the dying of Jesus ... for we who live are constantly being handed over to death for the sake of Jesus' (2 Cor 4:10f), he adds, 'therefore death works in us, but life in you.' By 'death' Paul understands his 'daily offering of his life': 'I die daily' (1 Cor 15:31). About this 'dying', by which the life of the community is increased, he says further, 'all things are for your sakes, so that the grace which is spreading over many may cause the giving of thanks to abound, to the glory of God' (2 Cor 4:15).

The spiritual life of the community is, therefore, dependent on Paul's sacrifice, on the reality of his following of Christ. Just as the death of Christ passes on life to us all, so also the dying of the Apostle means life for the community. This is true of the priest as well. Where a priest sacrifices himself for the community, there the community's growth in life is the fruit. The old saying, '*sanguis martyrum semen Christianorum*', the blood of the martyrs is the seed of new Christians, can be transferred to the priest with equal validity. One who wishes to win men for Christ must devote his own life by personal action and with sincere concern. Only a 'man of God' and a 'disciple of Christ' can carry out his official mission credibly and with fruit.

2. Priestly office is a service.

One of the great insights of the Second Vatican Council was to see and propose church office under the general heading of service. Office means service in two directions — for Christ and for the benefit of others. Regarded as service for Christ, it is essentially vicarious, as being merely a pointer, a transparent medium through which Christ can be seen (this has already been spoken of: p. 36 and *passim*): with regard to fellow Christians it can be exercised only through a life which is essentially lived for others. Basing itself on this insight, the Second Vatican Council has, as it were, given a new interpretation of the traditional image of official church power and authority. The sole meaning and content of 'hierarchical power' is service to others, 'so that even a single trace of arbitrary self-seeking or absolutist use of authority is a perversion of the concept of church office' (P.J. Cordes). Because Jesus Christ was among us as 'one who serves' (Lk 22:27), his official and sacramental representation must be carried out as a service (cf. Mt 20:25ff.). The ministry of Christ is more specifically described as *diakonia*, a word which basically means 'service at table'. But since in ancient times service at table was felt to be dishonourable, the work took on the pointed meaning of 'lowly service', the service of a slave. It is a service which involves becoming dirty: it counts for nothing and is despised by all. The corresponding noun *diakonos* came to have almost the same meaning as *doulos*, a slave. The mission of Christ was to a 'slave service' of this kind. Church office therefore cannot represent any other.

It is not surprising, therefore, that the New Testament, when speaking of church office, uses none of the words which were usual in the Greek linguistic and cultural sphere, all of which stress the element of power and supremacy. Only the one word is used instead — *diakonia*. Paul regards his apostolic office as a slave-service of this kind. He frequently describes himself as a 'slave of Christ', and also writes: 'I have made myself a slave for all, that I might win over more (1 Cor 9:19). A word which repeatedly occurs to describe the ministry for the community is *kopian*, to wear oneself out,' 'to work oneself to death'. That this word is to be taken in its full sense is clear, for example, from 1 Cor 4:11: 'To the present hour, we are hungry and thirsty, are poorly clothed, are subject to blows and are homeless ... we have become the scum of the world, the dregs of everything until now', and from many other passages (particularly, 2 Cor 11:23 ff.).

This concept of church office holds up a mirror to every priest: office in the Church can be exercised only as a humbling offer of oneself to service. It does not in any way justify any kind of personally privileged elite, any upper-class consciousness of rank and clerical black. Certainly God chooses people for special vocations. The whole of Scripture knows nothing of egalitarianism: there is selection, special position, special mission; but — and this puts everything in its proper place — a special vocation in Scripture always means the burden of a mission, to be a slave of others, to become stained in unprofitable ministries. A greater vocation involves a correspondingly greater burden and a greater humbling of the one who is called.

H. Urs v. Balthasar rightly says that in the New Covenant 'the ministry would not be a sign of Christ if the office which has been conferred does nor partake of the structure of his unique office, which essentially requires that the whole person is applied to the office. Is it, therefore, surprising that the whole care of the Lord in training his Apostles, particularly Peter, the Rock, for their office was aimed at making them humble? In the New Testament, the submerging of personality in the office, when rightly understood, simply means the greatest possible effort on the person's part to devote to the office everything that he has to give.... The effectiveness of the Catholic priest as an instrument of Christ derives from the effectiveness of Christ, which leads inevitably to the cross. Peter was relentlessly exercised in this.'

The priesthood of the New Testament, therefore, does not give entry to a special status, to an elite or super-caste. Instead it leads into unglamorous service. However, this service is not a reduction of church office to a sociological function or a clumsy denial of its theological basis (something which is not always avoided in many circles of so-called 'progressive' theology). Instead it frees from any 'ideology' the over-sacralised image of the priest which has come down from the past. St Augustine has expressed this concept of church office in these words: 'He who has set you (the community) free through his blood has made me your slave.' Therefore, the special characteristic of Church office is the vocation to be a slave.

Certainly this will involve very great and permanent spiritual demands, which can be met only when the service of the community is performed in an attitude of service for the Lord. The relationship to Jesus Christ frees one for a glad and serene community-service which is not self-seeking or self-celebrating, or which trusts one's own ability and sufficiency. When the priest is acting for Christ and representing him, then it is certainly the Lord himself who is acting in and through the commissioned disciple.

This simple conviction involves consequences for priestly spirituality, and for the form of church pastoral action, which could have explosive effects. For this is what it means: 'If the priest in his ministry is successful with people, then properly speaking it is God who is completing his saving action through his representative who is acting as a fellow-worker. And if the priest in spite of all his efforts does not succeed with those whom he serves, if his service is rejected, then once more it is God who (admittedly through his representative) is calling in vain for grace to be accepted' (R. Schulte). Is this not consolation enough? From this point of view, the ineffectiveness of everyday priestly work, which is experienced by many, the disappointment, frustration and the seeming unlikelihood of success in the future, must be viewed quite differently. The conviction that the priest is acting as a servant of Christ, and in his place, is surely something which takes a burden from his mind and imposes it on the Lord himself. He may in his official activity apply to himself the words of Jesus in the Gospel of St John, 'I am not doing anything on my own initiative: but I speak only as the Father taught me. And he who has sent me has not left me to be alone . . .' (Jn 8:28f.).

'He who has sent me, is with me!' It is not really the priest who has the care of souls, building up a community and passing on the salvific action of Christ; it is not he who is carrying on a church 'operation'; he probably may often think that this is what he is doing: if so, he is neglecting what really matters — the fact that God himself is acting through him in Jesus Christ and wishes to be heard and to act through the self-effacing action of the priest. The priest's position is like that of St John the Baptist, who was not the Light but merely gave testimony of the Light (cf. Jn 1:8). He is the 'friend of the bridegroom', who 'stands near' but leaves the wedding to the one to whom it belongs — Christ himself (cf. Jn 3:29). He is like the long outstretched finger of the Baptist on the Isenheimer altar: he is merely pointing to the one who is really carrying out his work of salvation through his representative. The fact that church office is an instrument is the fundamental reason why it is essentially service. Since it is God himself who is acting through the officials of the Church, they must 'continually keep before their minds the fact that they are beside God and in his service, a dignity which reaches its personal fulness if the person in question gives all the glory to God' (R. Schulte).

These truths are not new insights. But are they self-evidently the basic supports of priestly spirituality and action? With some office-bearers one can find a wrong attitude of two kinds which, though different, grow from the same root. Work in the Church is, as everyone knows, like filling a bottomless barrel. A thousand requests, demands, expectations are put to the priest from people needing help and seeking counsel, from the parish or from the diocesan chancery. Some priests respond with incredible activity, trying to fill this "bottomless barrel', usually feeling, however, that they are doing too little. The result is stress, activism, and 'a motor which is running idle'. The others become tired and resign themselves to attending only to what is absolutely necessary, since they see that they are permanently overstrained, and realise that it is impossible to do everything. Thus, on the one side there is hectic activity and on the other a resigned inertia. Both of these attitudes originate in the mistaken belief that the priest must be able to 'fix it'. However, it is not the priest who is acting, but Christ is acting through him. The community (or parish) is God's house, God's field (1 Cor 3:9), and not primarily the priest's field of work. The office of the priest, his service, is to work calmly with interior serenity and in obedience to the command of Christ, since he is the 'vicar' of him who will accomplish his own work.

This is also clear from the way in which Jesus Christ himself acted. Did he heal all the sick, console all the poor, feed all the hungry, set all men free from loneliness and isolation? Even he did not do everything! He has 'only' established signs, credible signs of the hope that what was then appearing in modest and small beginnings will be an universal reality one day, when God himself establishes his kingdom. If then the Lord has not done 'everything', why do office-bearers in the Church think that they must do 'everything'. Why cannot things be left undone, even if they seem to be still important in themselves? Instead, what is done should be done 'correctly', that is, in the spirit of Jesus, with his attitude, in such a way that he can shine through in the action of the priest.

The attitude of Jesus is particularly clear in the story of Zacchaeus (Lk 19:1 ff.). All Jericho ran to see Jesus, to hear his word, to witness his mighty signs. And what did he do? Instead of concerning himself with them all, he stood near one, Zacchaeus: 'Today I must be a guest in your house.' Jesus sees: this man needs me now! So he concentrates on this one, as if for him the others did not exist. How many must he disappoint, because he has to attend to the one real 'must', which proceeds from God's will. That is how Jesus acts: no widely extensive activity, no programme to reach all the individuals as far as possible, no full twenty-four hour service: he displays credible signs of hope, of love, of mercy. In the service of his Father, he does, without fuss, the 'one thing necessary', because he listens to the call of the hour, in which he finds the call of the Father.

It could be a test question for every priest, how he would have acted that day in Jericho. There is a Jericho everywhere, wherever there is pressure from people and pressure of work. Here the priest must also have the same priorities as Jesus — by listening to the call of the hour, to do the one thing necessary serenely and calmly in the knowledge that God is acting through him, now in small signs and stages, and eventually in such a way that he himself will bring about the universal kingdom. This conviction must create in us a quite different style of pastoral work, a style which is more spiritual and serene, and above all it must bring us more joy — that joy which so often is missing in busy holders of church office.

The problem which this poses may soon become even more urgent. The level of pastoral practice still being carried on today cannot continue indefinitely. In the coming years there will probably be fewer priests. Must they nevertheless continue to do an ever-increasing amount of work, subject themselves to growing stress, and try to 'muddle on', often feeling joyless and tired? And would it be possible with a good conscience to seek for candidates for a calling of this kind? If no other arguments prevail, at least future developments compel us to make a fundamental change of direction. Some spheres of activity will simply have to be abandoned, even with the clear knowledge that they are at times most important. The official duty of hearing the confessions of hundreds of schoolchildren, the compulsory celebration of numberless Masses, the preparation — often superficial through lack of time — of sermons and religious instruction, the 'guest-appearance' of the priest at meetings of clubs and groups: what should all these lead to, if it is no longer possible to allow Christ to appear convincingly in them and to guide people in following him and in the expectation of his kingdom? What would be the sense of pastoral activity if it is not directed to what is essential?

Many holders of church office are ceaselessly concerned about quantity and number, about what one can see and count. But number, quantity, measurable success are not categories to be found in Holy Scripture. 'Success is not one of God's names' (M. Buber). Neither the large or the small flock is the ideal: what matters is to help people to follow Christ's example and to prepare a community of the Lord. Therefore, the priest must stand in the community first of all as a spiritual man. He must be present for men in a spiritual manner, that is, as one guided by the Gospel and in a personal relationship with the Lord. He must do what he can and as far as he can: and do it convincingly, with joy, in devotion to the Lord and with complete readiness to serve the community. It is not organisation that does this, or big numbers, or statistics. How can the slave expect visible and measurable success if the Lord experienced failure on the cross? The priestly office must preserve its character of service even by renouncing visible success.

3. One of the community and distinct from it

This third main support of priestly spirituality is also derived from the essential nature of church office. Because he is an official representative of Christ, the priest is distinct from the community. As one Christian among Christians, indeed as a fellow-Christian in whom the Church is represented in a special way, he is a member of the community. The resulting basic tension is of the essence of priestly ministry. 'When at the *hanc igitur* in the Roman Canon of the Mass the priest stretches out his hands over the gifts to symbolise the fact that they are the offering of the Church, he is acting as a member of the liturgical assembly, for which he is making the offering. He is, however, a commissioned member and symbolically represents the assembly. On the other hand, at the moment when the Last Supper is made present, the priest who repeats the words and gestures of Jesus is a figure and symbol of Christ the Mediator of the New Covenant' (P. Colin). Throughout the whole history of theology, the concept of church office is marked by this fundamental tension: *in the community* as one of its (commissioned) members, and *distinct from the community*, as a sign of Christ. This is noted, for example, in such recent documents as the decree of the Second Vatican Council on the priesthood (no. 3) and Pope John Paul II's first Holy Thursday letter.

This fundamental tension, which should not be removed, always involves something like a journey along a difficult mountain ridge (or a kind of tight-rope walking). In the Church the danger has always existed that one pole would be overstressed at the cost of the other. Before Vatican II the emphasis was put on the distinction of the priest from the community, his 'otherness'. This emphasis was often exaggerated, a danger which has never been absent, especially in clerically minded circles, and which is increasing again at present. Nevertheless, in the first years after that Council, so much stress was put on the 'in the community' aspect, particularly by younger priests, that the special and specific aspect of church office was in danger of being obscured.

In the everyday life of the priest, there is no general solution for dealing with this tension. Nevertheless, a kind of general rule can be of some help: since at the important moments of church life, while proclaiming the word, celebrating the sacraments and engaged in pastoral counselling, the priest is distinct from the community as a representative of Christ and is acting with spiritual authority. But when he is not officially performing sacramental actions, he should rather withdraw to the background in order to make it more obvious that he is a member of the community together with his fellow Christians. When, therefore, his spiritual authority, granted him by the Lord, is not being exercised, the office-bearer must renounce all distinction and regard himself, even in community decisions, as *one* member of the community, as one Christian among fellow Christians.

It is not easy to see, therefore, why in community decisions on such things as flower decoration in the church, the building of a kindergarten, the furnishing of a club for senior citizens, official spiritual authority should have a role, and why the priest should have more influence in the making of such decisions than the parish council or lay experts.

Against this it might be objected that the priest is, after all, still a priest even if he is not carrying out official functions. That is true in a sense: the grace given in ordination is a charisma which is permanent, as 2 Tim 1:6 tells us (see also 1 Tim 4:14). To be a priest is to be more than a functionary: the one ordained is taken by Christ into permanent service. But the presence of Christ in the office-bearer through the sacramental sign is not to be thought of as a static substantial presence which makes the priest essentially an *alter Christus* and makes his official authority something which is a personal possession of his own. Instead, the salvific activity of Christ is mediated through him in actions which are sacramental signs: his authority is attached to the actions, his sacramental representation of Christ takes place in definite sacramental 'situations' — preaching the word, administering the sacraments, leading the community towards a life of the imitation of Christ.

At the Second Vatican Council, some voices warned of a possible misunderstanding of the priest's representation of Christ as something essentially ontological. The formulae chosen for the decree on the ministry and life of priests — for example that the priest has the ability 'to act in the person of Christ the head' (*Presbyterorum ordinis*, no. 2) — are intended to emphasise that his sacramental 'representation of Christ' is related to his action. Certainly his power to act is grounded in something real. But this reality — St Thomas Aquinas describes it as a *potentia* or a *habitus*, a potency or capacity to act — is actuated in determinate sacramental rites.[21] That is also clearly the view of another doctor of the Church, St Robert Bellarmine: he expressly restricts *in persona Christi* to the priest's official sacramental actions. He says, for example: 'Hence Christ offers the sacrifice through one who is inferior, the Church offers through one who is superior. That is to say, the priest inasmuch as he is an offerer is superior to the people, and in this he is not a servant of the Church but a servant of Christ, the primary Mediator.' In this passage representation of Christ is restricted in two ways: to the extent that Christ makes his sacrifice present through the ministry of the priest, the priest is 'superior' to the people, and he is not a minister of the Church but of Christ, in relation to his special sacramental activity. It is, therefore, only in certain determinate actions that he as office-bearer is distinct from the rest of the people of God.[22] From this point of view, one must critically examine many clerical differences of rank, beginning with pseudo-hierarchical titles and special forms of clerical dress,[23] then certain kinds of house and lifestyle, and finally special positions and privileges in society. For this examination the criticism of office-bearers in St Matthew, chapter 23 will always present a norm and a challenge: 'Do not be called Rabbi, for one is your teacher and you are all brothers. Do not be called teachers, for one is your teacher, O Christ. But the greatest among you shall be your servant.'

This ideal applies to the holder of church office even when he is acting with official authority and sacramentally distinct from the community. As we can learn from the Pauline epistles, the greatest efforts must be made to bring about the involvement of the entire community in agreement and consensus. St Paul speaks in different ways 'of the limitations which he himself has set upon the use of his authority' (H. Schlier). To be sure, he can also threaten a 'naked use of his authority, if the community by its criticism of authority would have fallen away from the ecclesial *communio* of obedience in faith and love. But he regards such a situation as an extreme case which is basically impossible and which would reveal a failure of the Church — the breakup of the *communio* which according to him maintains its intrinsic structure through an authority which lives according to the model of Christ' (H. Urs v. Balthasar).

And finally: even when the priest must oppose the rest of the community, he will not be in a dangerous and self-centred independence: instead he will be, according to ancient ecclesiastical tradition, in the network of the 'presbyterium', together with other office-bearers (especially the bishops). To them he must render an account of his official ministry (cf. also pp. 161ff).

6

Central points of spirituality

The basic spiritual attitudes dealt with in the previous section take concrete form in particular aspects of priestly work.

1. *Pastoral ministry in practice*

The first great — and fundamental — field of action for the spirituality of the priest is the pastoral ministry to which he has been assigned. In general, this involves the gathering and building up the Christian community, by the proclamation of the word and the celebration of the sacraments, as well as by guiding them in liturgy, mission and service. However, the task assigned and the actual situation will in each case determine more precisely its content and its focal point. Pastoral ministry takes one shape for a parish priest, and another for a hospital chaplain or a professor of theology: but it is always a specific sacramental representation of 'Christ's service', of his work for the salvation of mankind. Consequently, every priestly ministry is centred in the celebration of the Eucharist, in which the unconditional love of the Father and the sacrifice of Christ are guaranteed to us and made sacramentally visible. Moreover, it causes the faithful to be accepted in the Holy Spirit into the salvific action of God, and to celebrate this action with thanksgiving and praise, being thus enabled to live in reconciliation and peace with God and among themselves. All pastoral activity must ultimately aim at this central reality of the Eucharist, if it is not to go off into irrelevancies. But the roads to this objective can be many, and therefore priestly ministry can take many concrete forms. Last but not least, it depends on the 'human' abilities of the priest: indeed it requires them. Since the

Eucharist is intended to effect unity of Christians with Christ and among themselves, the ministry which aims at this unity 'presupposes a certain suitability for this task — ability to establish contact with people and converse with them, care for the needs and happiness of others, the human gift of the ability to preside over a community and to lead it, while respecting its freedom, (including a talent for organisation). All this requires a unifying, peaceable and reconciling nature and for this it is necessary to have some knowledge of people, a sure judgment, an unprejudiced outlook, ability to communicate, initiative and imagination' (W. Kaspar).

Although such characteristics are also gifts of God's grace, human effort still has a part to play (see pp. 128ff). Every effort to acquire truly human virtues and attitudes is for the priest at the same time part of his pastoral ministry. St Paul's words are to the point: 'We do not give offence to anyone, lest our ministry be discredited'(2 Cor 6:3); anyone who gives offence as a man is hindering his ministry as a priest. Still more: without a 'human infrastructure', pastoral ministry is in danger of lapsing into empty ritual or irrelevant 'uplift'. In its human demeanour not only is the credibility of the official ministry at stake. but also the *reality* of the sacramentally transmitted salvation. For example, baptism of an individual also denotes his incorporation into the Church: but this *real* incorporation already begins in the way in which the parish priest receives the parents when they come to arrange for a child's baptism. Similarly, the official proclamation of the Gospel is part of the greater totality of daily conversation, and the official guidance of the community depends on the human demeanour of the parish priest towards his fellowmen. The proclamation of the word, the administration of the sacraments and (in the strict sense) the guidance of the community are, therefore, not the only elements of priestly ministry.

This point is emphasised by Klaus Hemmerle in quite characteristic fashion:

I am thinking of quite ordinary services — helping someone, giving a present, being available, having some time to spare for others, perhaps sometimes doing some service for another, a service for which we have not been ordained, but which is simply something which any neighbour, if he is a Christian, must do for his neighbour. To me this seems to be something very important for the priest.

I am constantly thankful that I have also things to do — not only things that priests have to do — but quite simple things which are trivial or onerous or bureaucratic. Obviously, I think it is good to be reasonably orderly and plan the way I spend my time: but it is important in my life as a priest that I do not simply tick off my own duties, becoming like a mere 'functionary'. On the contrary, it is important that I carry out my Christian ministry in concrete service of others and being available for others. I must accept the strains of daily life, and the trivial monotony of human concerns, not indeed as a manager or organiser, but as one who serves. I ought to wash the feet of others, not just once on Holy Thursday, but on that Holy Thursday which is always present.

The ministry of the priest also has social and political dimensions. Admittedly, the greatest care must be taken here. The priest (or a community or a local church) must not permit a takeover by a particular political party, a pressure group, a vocational group and above all by the 'climate' of a particular social order (whether conservative or 'progressive'). Such a takeover would create the danger that corresponding political commitment on the Church's part would amount to giving a blessing to special interests, and that particular social structures and activities would be legitimated by ecclesiastical approval. Consequently, in the political sphere the discernment of spirits is specially needed. This is true for every individual Christian and every Christian community: it is above all true for the priest. As representing Christ, he should be a sign of that — rightly understood — non-partisan attitude which Jesus himself maintained. Jesus refused to intervene in legal conflicts (Lk 12:13 ff), to issue political value judgments (Lk 13:1 ff). Instead he directed attention to the 'one thing necessary'.

Certainly there have been, and still are, political situations in which the Church and the authorities of the Church must, with courage and vigour, issue against social evil its declaration 'That you may not do!' In appropriate instances the Church must translate this into action, when human dignity, the liberty of God's children, and the good order of creation are at risk. But when this situation does not arise the holder of church office must draw back and leave concrete political decisions to 'political judgment' made where possible in the light of faith. This by no means involves lack of interest in matters of social policy: for 'the Church, and especially the priest, will not become socially relevant by repeating

156 CENTRAL POINTS OF SPIRITUALITY

in somewhat different and more impressive words what many others are already saying, and often saying much better. The priest will be socially relevant above all when he carries out his independent ministry, which belongs to him alone. The kind of political ministry proper to the priest is to speak of God. It is as a man of faith and of prayer that he can be a light and strength for the laity in the ministry entrusted to them in the world' (W. Kaspar).

The pastoral ministry is not only the specific life-task of the priest. It is also the way and the means of his personal sanctification (cf. *Presbyterorum ordinis*, no. 13). In his pastoral activity he should at the same time come closer to the goal of all spiritual endeavour: to find God in all things, to seek to discover in all the demands, events and situations of his pastorate the self-giving love of God. This love requires from the priest an answering love which takes concrete form in the service of the flock entrusted to him. Following this line of thought the Second Vatican Council recognised in the concept of *caritas pastoralis*, 'pastoral love', the 'bond of priestly perfection . . . which will unify the lives of priests and their activity. Therefore, they will achieve unity in their lives by uniting themselves with Christ in acknowledging the Father's will and their offer of themselves on behalf of the flock entrusted to them' (*Presbyterorum ordinis*, no. 14). Christ wishes his pastoral love to be present and continue in the pastoral love of the priest.

2. Prayer

When conversation ceases, a relationship ceases. So it is among men, and the same applies between God and man. Prayer is therefore an essential part of the life of faith. Prayer expresses and makes actual our relationship with God. Prayer is 'faith speaking' (O.H. Pesch). This is true of every believer, but is has special significance for the priest, since he is drawn by his mission into a particular relationship with the one who sent him. That is why the priest, at his ordination, also takes on an obligation to recite the prayer of the hours. However, if anyone thought that this was enough, he would be quite mistaken. Important as the prayer of the Breviary is, it 'lives' by the fact that it is founded on personal prayer. Without long, persevering and personal prayer, the fixed form stiffens into an empty, dead formality, which ultimately one goes through and gets finished with, or to which one turns only 'when one feels like it'. A personal relationship requires personal prayer — and this can be very demanding: in prayer the believer experiences not only the loving nearness of God, but also that He seems to be absent and hidden.

When we are ready to pray, God does not come as it were automatically into the world of our experience, to satisfy our search for him with his consolation and to meet our weakness with his strength. He is not a kind of an idol which we can summon up in prayer for our spiritual self-satisfaction. God is the Being who is 'completely Other', who is hidden and who withdraws himself. For this reason, prayer does not quench our thirst for life-fulfilment by God: in fact, it increases it: our unsatisfied longing will be fully satisfied only in the kingdom of God. Until then prayer means seeking God in faith, silent waiting, persevering action, without ever being able to find him completely. Inevitably, a point comes when we feel we cannot bear prayer, silence, aloneness. We realise that achievement, action, talking, making a noise, dwelling on our own thoughts, wishes, and imagination, are much more congenial than prayer, recollection and silent waiting in the presence of God. Prayer, in a word, is unsatisfying. And already there is the strong temptation to abandon it and to spend the time in doing other, 'more sensible', things, activities which produce more results — instead of kneeling silent and unsatisfied before God. How many people, on account of such an experience, abandon personal prayer or relegate it to the second or third place! There are more than enough 'alibis' for acting in this way with a good conscience — the pressure of pastoral work, constant interruptions, countless duties. Many priests consequently say, 'My work is a prayer!', and feel released from a burdensome duty: the necessary tension between prayer and work is resolved in favour of work.

This tension between prayer and apostolic work can be seen in the life of Jesus (cf. Mk 1:35 ff). His disciples also are called 'to be with him' (Mk 3:14) just as much as to be sent on a mission of preaching. It continues throughout the history of the Church and especially in the lives of the saints. What this means is that prayer and work, contemplation and action, the desert and apostolic vocation in the world presuppose each other, forming a unity which certainly is under tension: nevertheless, they are interdependent. Every mission from God into the world begins with listening to his word and responding to it, and in constantly renewing this 'dialogue'. It is only when pastoral activity is founded upon contemplation that it does not lose sight of its proper goal of leading the community entrusted to it into a personal relationship with God which is particularly expressed in prayer. For this reason Joshua was instructed 'to meditate on the law of the Lord day and night, that you may act according to it'(Josh 1:8).

Prayer provides an important criterion for a priest's understanding of himself. It brings up a basic question: How does he see himself — as a pastoral 'manager' or as a man of God, as a mere 'functionary' or as one who does his work in union with Christ? Without prayer, pastoral care eventually becomes superficial and at best distorted into a business operation. A priest who does not pray becomes unable to recognise what is essential, and consequently fails to notice God's call in daily life: his words and action do not derive from listening to God's word. A bishop once said, 'I need to listen only two or three minutes to a priest's sermon, and then I know if he prays'. Does not the community also notice this?

To be sure, there are also those duties and appointments in the pastor's daily work which so often overwhelm his good intention to pray. But do not many priests react to this in a very illogical way? For example, when teaching in a school is involved, when he takes on commitments for lectures, seminars, church services, a priest will usually make a note of those appointments and keep them at all costs. Why are the times for prayer not also noted down in the same kind of way and treated in exactly the same was as his other obligations? If this does not happen, if prayer is the first thing dropped from one's daily programme, it is clearly not the many duties that are responsible for the omission, but a wrong scale of values.

Above all, the priest must keep in mind that prayer is not merely his own individual concern. It belongs to the duties he owes to the people entrusted to him, and this under three aspects:

a) The office-bearer in the Church has to deal with many people for whom God is immensely distant, obscure, dead. In his personal prayer he will certainly experience for himself the darkness of faith and thus take his stand in solidarity with those who find faith difficult. Together with them he experiences in his own body, so to speak, the struggle to reach God: 'I will not let you go, until you bless me' (Gen 32:26). This testimony of his search for God in prayer — often imperfect — will thus be a testimony for others also, and is therefore part of his mission.

b) The community has a right to a pastor who is not constantly taking refuge in activity, thus running away from himself. Instead they have a right to one who 'faces up to' God and himself. They do not need just a 'validly ordained' priest, but one who is also a 'man of God', who throughout his life listens to God, who comes to them as such and is available for them. How else should priests fulfil the instructions of the Second Vatican Council: 'The duty of priests is to teach, not their own ideas, but at all times God's word (*Presbyterorum ordinis*, no. 4).

c) Already in the Old Testament an essential task of the 'men of God' was to come before God as representatives of the others and cast themselves into the balance on their behalf. Thus they kept a place for God in the midst of a people which often enough shut itself up against him and denied him. In this line of men of God, which also includes Jesus, is the priest. He is required to pray as a representative of others. He — certainly in union with other Christians — is a kind of permanent 'delegate for prayer' on behalf of the community. Many of the faithful instinctively take this for granted: they come to the priest and say, 'Pray for me!' Many others do not ask this explicitly but nevertheless they expect it to be done.

The priest must therefore very seriously reflect on the quality of his personal prayer; should he devote a longer time to daily prayer, a time which is not dependent on the whim of the moment. As Karl Rahner says, 'the faith of to-day's priest is the faith of a priest who prays — one could almost say, who practises mystical contemplation. Otherwise it is nothing.'

3. Study and spiritual reading

The priest is ordained for the ministry of the word. As Christ's representative, he must pass on the Gospel of the kingdom. But it must come to men as a credible and stirring message. The decree of the Second Vatican Council on the priesthood says that 'in order to touch the spirit and heart of the hearers, God's word must not be presented only in generalities and abstractly. The eternal truths of the Gospel must be applied to the concrete circumstances of life. Accordingly, the ministry of the word is exercised in different ways, according to the needs of the hearers and the talents of the preachers' (*Presbyterorum ordinis*, no. 4). The Council means that the word should not be preached 'any old way', but in such a way that it can reach the actual hearer at that particular moment. This calls for reflection, effort, study — especially nowadays, when people come to the Gospel with numerous questions and problems, and frequently with an attitude of critical scepticism. The preaching of the faith has to take up people's problems and meet their critical questions with rational arguments.

This is impossible without study, and to this extent it is an indispensable duty of the priest.

The following example may help to show the need for study. A surgeon who does not keep up with professional developments can perform unsuccessful operations due to his lack of knowledge of new discoveries and techniques. He can be sued for professional negligence. What is to be said of a priest who, because he has neglected to study, similarly offends in his preaching against his duty of pastoral care, and fails to reach his parishioners by his preaching and instruction about the faith, with the result that the word of God cannot develop its full force?

In his Holy Thursday message in 1979 John Paul II emphatically recommended further study: 'It is not enough to stand still with the knowledge we acquired in the seminary. Our intellectual develoment must continue right through life. . . . For the sake of mankind we must be suitably qualified witnesses to Jesus Christ. As teachers of the truth and the moral law, it is our task to give a convincing and effective account of the hope which fills us. This also is part of our daily conversion to love through the truth.' For the Pope, therefore, study is linked with daily conversion. It involves a real effort which must be made every day, and is therefore a central point of priestly spirituality.

Something similar is true of spiritual reading, which gives spiritual stimulation. It is specially the one appointed to transmit the faith who is always in need of new stimuli, to make sure that he is not like a motor being 'raced' in neutral, that is, uttering commonplace and meaningless clichés. Even his own life of faith cannot continue to be supported by 'route-march rations' carried in a haversack which he packed during his seminary days to last for his whole life. Everyone changes in the course of time. The situations of life and work change. New questions and attitudes arise. Insights and attitudes once considered obvious become problematic. It is self-deception to think that one can successfully work out every problem by oneself. That is to overlook the fact that all of us live as well — and to a considerable degree — out of the experiences, insights and ideas of others. For this reason the priest — and obviously others also — in addition to spiritual intercourse with others, needs spiritual reading, as a kind of permanent spritual companion. One of the great English spiritual directors of priests, Ronald Knox, remarks in a chapter about tepidity: 'If you ask me for a remedy against it, my short answer is: "Spiritual Reading".'

It may be asked why their parishioners receive so little stimulation from so many priests, why so many sermons are so unfruitful and so shallow, so full of clichés. Is it because the priest himself receives too little stimulation?

4. Priests among themselves and working with each other

It is well known that lasting difficulties can arise among priests. *Invidia clericalis*, jealousy about the success of another priest, is — to put it bluntly — proverbial. The relationship of parish priest and curate (a particular instance of the 'generation gap') is not infrequently subject to tension. But such difficulties do occur in other comparable works of life and should not be overestimated. True, the question is sometimes asked why 'spiritual men', who are conscious of a divine call to follow Christ in a special manner, are not mature enough to meet the demands of such situations. But we need not discuss this here. On the other hand, a theological exposition of church office must emphasise that this official mission, as it began in the New Testament and continued to develop in the history of the Church, is essentially communitarian.

Very early on Jesus sent out his disciples two by two, so that they might give witness as a 'college' to the kingdom of God, in word and in action. He called them to leave their families, their 'old' human relationships and at the same time set them into the new family of his brothers and sisters. This 'collegiality' of the disciples may perhaps have first shown itself when they all 'with one mind' ran way at the sight of his failure (Mt 26:56). At any rate, they were given a new unanimity in their vocation by the Holy Spirit (Acts 2:1ff), an unanimity which would fundamentally persist in the Church. Thus St Paul, in the passage which is important for showing his concept of office in the Church (2 Cor 5; cf. p. 33ff above) uses the first person plural: we, apostles: we, sent to represent Christ. The ecumenical conversations of the Dombes Group on the subject of 'Le ministère épiscopal' gives this brief outline of the New Testament situation: 'The pastors of the different Churches exercise their ministry in solidarity. The New Testament gives instructions for mutual fraternal visits (Acts 21:17-18; Gal 2:1-10), for exchange of letters (Col 4:16), for sending office-bearers to newly founded communities (Acts 11:19-26; 13:1-3), for collecting alms for churches in need (2 Cor 8:9), for mutual discussion so as to reach joint conclusions (Act 15:1-35).' In addition, the ultimate Jewish origin of the title of *presbyter* contains a reminder of its collegiate structure: a *presbyter* is a member of a *presbyterium*.

These few indications point in a quite definite direction: namely, that the special ministry of representing Christ needs itself incorporation in a common body — the priest in the *presbyterium*, the bishop in the episcopal college. Certainly, the primary purpose of the collegial structure of church office is to set each single community or diocese, represented by its leader, into the totality of the Church of which it is a part. But collegiality also means that the individual office-bearer comes before the community a a person who is incorporated in the fraternal group of the officially appointed disciples of Christ and so points to their Lord and Master who is the source and goal of all brotherliness.

The fraternal character of church office needs to be more intensively put in practice, particularly today. In a society which is becoming ever more 'worldly', the priest needs a closer personal connection with, and a lifestyle marked by, fraternal and friendly relationships in which he can live as a Christian and a priest. Jesus did not call his disciples to leave their families in order to isolate them, but in order to introduce them into his 'new family'. This 'new family' is certainly in the first place the community (or parish) of which he is in charge, and in which he is one Christian among fellow Christians. But are our communities really spheres of common life? What we call a community is often much too large, too difficult to see as a whole, too anonymous to be the basis and support of a living community. There is often missing the infrastructure necessary for the development of a shared life. Infrastructures of this kind could be family and neighbourhood groups, spiritual groups, discussion circles and action teams of various kinds. It is only where a community is recognisable as a 'family of God' that it is a community which makes it possible to follow the way of Jesus, a sphere in which one bears another's burdens. Only in this way can the community be a protecting environment for the priest as well. Otherwise the crisis of the community becomes a crisis for the priest also.

But the priest in his community is not only a Christian among fellow Christians. He is also one of the group of the other specially commissioned disciples. Is this only an ideal, or is it a reality?

The decree of the Second Vatican Council cites many reasons for fraternal solidarity among priests:

Older priests should accept younger priests as being truly their brothers and stand by them in the first works and initial difficulties of their ministry. They should also try to understand their mentality, different though it may be, and willingly help to foster their initiatives. Similarly, young priests should make sure they respect the age and experience of older priests, discuss pastoral problems with them and cooperate willingly with them. The spirit of brotherly love imposes an obligation on priests to cultivate hospitality, to do good and to share their goods with one another. They should have particular care for priests who are sick, hard pressed, overburdened with work, lonely, exiled, and those who are suffering persecution. They should also be glad to meet one another for the sake of recreation, remembering the words spoken by the Lord when he invited the tired apostles, "Come away by yourselves and rest for a while" (Mk 6:31). Furthermore, in order that priests may be mutually helped in their spiritual life and in widening the range of their knowledge, and to enable them to cooperate more fruitfully in their ministry and be better protected from dangers which may threaten one who is living alone, community life of some sort is to be fostered among them. . . . Finally, their common association in the priesthood should lead them to realise that they have a particular obligation to those who are labouring under any kind of difficulty. . . . With brotherly love and great generosity of heart they should stand ready to help those who have failed in some way, and intercede for them with God in urgent prayer, while continually showing themselves to them as true brothers and friends (*Presbyterorum ordinis*, no. 8).

But is there not a need for more binding forms of common living and joint pastoral action? Above all, how can a life of celibacy for the sake of God's kingdom be successfully lived and lead to maturity, without the atrophy of human values such as friendliness, ability to communicate and to express emotions etc? The Church cannot demand celibacy without creating the conditions required for its practice. Can, may, one seek to gain a young man for the priesthood without offering him at the same time a form of life which is convincing, humanly and spiritually possible, attractive? Does not the present-day mode of life of priests discourage many a person from adopting this vocation, because he feels he would be left to 'roost' somewhere, alone and isolated? Here and there are to be found different kinds of societies of priests, pastoral teams, and a form of life in community. Nevertheless, the full importance of the problem has not been recognised — never mind solved — by many bishops and priests. It would go beyond the limits of this book to discuss models of life for priests. But one thing is certain: a priest can be a representative of Christ in the full sense only if he carries on his ministry in association with his fellow office-bearers.

From this requirement a series of questions arise about the spiritual life of the office-bearer. Why is the life of many a priest an isolated life? Why is cooperation among priests so difficult? In a time when priests are needed and pastoral work grows more burdensome, can it be afforded that a priest be a 'one man army'? (although there will always be vocations of this kind). Why is a helpful spiritual conversation between priests often so very difficult? Surely there must be very much to say and to contribute — sharing dificulties, exchanging suggestions, and above all, encouraging another. St Paul did not hesitate to confess that, amid the difficulties and trials of his ministry, he was consoled by the communities, his fellow Christians, and above all by his apostolic fellow workers (cf. e.g. 2 Cor 7:6 ff). Mutual fraternal consolation is a continuation of that which comes from God himself (cf. 2 Cor 1:3ff).

5. Concern to provide successors

Already in the New Testament there are indications that the office-bearer must exert himself to provide a successor to himself in his ministry. For a long time it was an 'unwritten law' among the clergy that each should be able to say of one young man at least that if he had not helped him to the priesthood, he had at any rate accompanied him on the way to it. The second Vatican Council points to this duty: since it cannot be expected that vocation to the priesthood is given to young men in an extraordinary manner, the vocation 'is to be perceived and judged from the signs by which the will of God is usually made known to prudent Christians. These signs must be carefully observed by priests' (*Presbyterorum ordinis*, no. 11).

In fact, God normally issues his call through men, and the priest must ask himself if God does not wish to awaken through him the readiness of a young man to accept his call. Life begins from life. The desire to become a priest is awakened by the sight of a priesthood exercised in exemplary fashion. Such a priest must be concerned about possible successors, even explicitly drawing attention for the need for successors. Not a few priests today neglect this, and some even quite deliberately reject it. Some openly say why they do: because they do not feel happy and fulfilled in their ministry, they wish to spare others a journey along this road. That is at least an honest attitude. However, others avoid speaking to young men about vocations to the spiritual life, especially to the priesthood, because they feel they may be infringing on essential freedom of choice.

A glance at the history of the Church will show that there was not such 'hypersensitivity' in early times. In antiquity suitable young men were urged to become priests to such an extent that many a suitable man took care to keep out of the way of bishops and communities that were looking for priests (the best-known example of this is St Augustine). Among monks (who were laymen) the principle was actually current, 'Avoid women and bishops!' so as not to yield to either of these different forms of enticements, which would involve giving up the monastic life. In fact, in Christian antiquity it was taken as normal that a person be (morally) compelled to accept ordination (which did not mean that a fundamental consent to ordination was not required). On the other hand, people were sceptical and had reservations about anyone who was over-anxious to seek ordination. It was not the continual thought, 'Have I a vocation or not?', or the personal decision of a young man to go forward, that was regarded as a sign of God's call. Instead, it was external pressure, especially pressure from a community, and in view of the predicament of the community which had to have a priest, the young man usually yielded to this pressure, even if not quite enthusiastically.

Could not this practice of the early Church contain some suggestions for our time? If no sermons are preached about the meaning of and need for the priesthood, if priests and parishes do not point out to the young clearly and emphatically that they are needed and that they can also count upon the support of all, is it not surprising that the omens are not good for the next generation of priests? We should, moreover, consider the fact that nowadays young men are not infrequently very lacking in individual self-confidence — more than in the past. Many of them are almost unable to say to themselves: 'I should like to become a priest!' They have not the necessary self-confidence. For this very reason, they need encouragement and confirmation from others. They need someone to say to them: 'I think that you are capable of that! You would be able for that!' Nevertheless preaching about the ministry and conversation with the young do call for tact. This is not only a matter of good manners: as the faith teaches, it is God himself who issues the call, and it does not come from the importunity of men.

Concern to provide for successors is a part of the essential nature of church office. Every office-bearer takes his place in the apostolic succession, and himself needs a successor. But if life takes its origin from life, the priest must ask himself: Does my priestly life attract others to offer themselves to that life?

Instead of an epilogue:
Ten principles for a priest's life pattern[24]

W. Breuning and K. Hemmerle

1. How I live as a priest is more important than what I do as a priest.

2. What Christ does through me is more important than what I do by myself.

3. It is more important for me to live in union with the presbyterium than to be alone and absorbed in my work.

4. The ministry of prayer and the word is more important than serving at tables.

5. It is more important to work united with my fellow workers than to do the maximum number of jobs all by myself.

6. It is more important to concentrate on a few points and to influence others, than to be hurried and incomplete in everything.

7. Joint action is more important than isolated action, no matter how perfect. Thus cooperation in work is more important than work, *communio* more important than action.

8. The cross is more important than efficiency: it is more fruitful.

9. Openness to the whole (community, diocese, Church throughout the world) is more important than a particular interest, no matter how important that may be.

10. It is more important that the faith be witnessed to all, than that all 'traditional' demands be satisfied.

Notes

1 This change of emphasis is due to an exchange of meaning of the two concepts *corpus Christi mysticum* and *corpus Christi verum* in the twelfth century. Originally *corpus Christi mysticum* was applied to the Eucharist, and *corpus Christi verum* to the Church. Both concepts were now interchanged. Consequently, the office-bearer who was originally ordained for the *corpus Christi verum* (= for the service of the Church) was now primarily related to the new interpretation of the *corpus Christi verum* (= the Eucharist).

2 This is now to some extent conceded by Protestant exegetes also. See H. Schütte, *Amt, Ordination und Sukzession . . .* (Düsseldorf 1974) 44ff. See also the agreed Dombes declaration in *Herder Korrespondenz* 27 (1973) 38: By means of the official ministry, Christ leads 'his disciples to spiritual sacrifice, to witness, and to ministry, along manifold paths which meet in the Eucharist. In this sense the official ministry is called sacerdotal'.

3 According to Jas 1:27, love and care for the defenceless and the needy, and a rejection of the world of sin, are particularly a part of the priestly ministry of sacrifice. Nevertheless, this 'practical' divine service is not to be contrasted to the cultic ministry, 'but to a theoretical and programmatic Christianity (cf. Jas 2:22 ff). The practical priestly ministry of the people of God is nowhere opposed to the cultic ministry of the sacrifice of praise and the Eucharist. The theory that the ministry of the people of God is carried out only in "the daily life of the world" has no foundation in the New Testament. Naturally it is also carried out there, to the extent that life in the world gives continual opportunity and summons to practical love. But the cult, the common divine service of the assembled people of God among whom "the death of the Lord is proclaimed" and his sacrifice made present, it is this cult which arouses the true and active love of the neighbour which will assist all the poor and helpless': Schlier, *Der priesterliche Dienst*, I (Freiburg-Basle-Vienna 1970) 98 ff.

4 This is the unanimous conviction of Catholic theologians. Even 'progressive' theologians agree. Cf. e.g. Schillebeeckx in *Diak.* I (1970) 149. There is also widespread agreement in ecumenical conversations about church office. See on this Schütte, op. cit. 48 ff; H. Meyer in *Theologischer Konsens und Kirchenspaltung* (ed. P. Lengsfeld and H. G. Stobbe, Stuttgart 1981) 24 ff. Similarly the agreed statement of the Catholic-Lutheran Commission, *Das Geistliche Amt in der Kirche* (Paderborn-Frankfurt 1981) 23: 'For the right understanding of church office, it is fundamental for Lutherans and Catholics that church office is both distinct from the community and also a part of the community'.

5 This aspect is emphasised in the two agreed statements of the Dombes Group

(cf. *Her-Korr* 27. 1973, 33-39). The authorised leaders, who must represent the Lord sacramentally, make clear at the same time 'that the assembly is not in control of the rite which it is in fact performing, that it is not lord over the Eucharist: it receives the Eucharist from another, from Christ, who continues to live in his Church' (1, IX 34).

*A contribution by E. Schlink and others to the *Memorandum* of the working party of the ecumenical institutes of the University of Munich (Mainz 1973), 176.

6 J. Ratzinger, in *Das Neue Volk Gottes* (Düsseldorf 1969) 106, sees this as the essential difference from the Protestant conception. In the Churches of the Reformation 'a kind of personification of the word takes place. It is conceived of as an entity which manifests itself as something independent of and distinct from the Church, and is seen as an independent and pre-existing standard to which the Church must conform. In this way the problem was outlined which has remained without change to the present day. Evangelical theology defines the Church in isolation from church office, and sets the word as an independent corrective for the official Church. Catholic theology on the other hand regards the official Church as the criterion of the word. It does not recognise an independent quasi-personified word which is distinct from the Church. On the contrary, for it the word lives on in the Church, just as the Church lives from the word — a relation of reciprocal dependence and connection. This may in fact be true of some tendencies in Evangelical theology, but on the other hand there are quite different opinions in Evangelical Christianity. See the summary of theological positions and official declarations of the VELKD in Schütte, op. cit. 62.

7 For Thomas the fundamental essence of the ministry of service is precisely that this 'instrument' is purely a tool. Cf. *Summa theologica* III, 61, 1: 'Eadem ratio est ministri et instrumenti'.

8 Even the distinction of Jesus from the Father, which is characterised by obedience, is elevated by the Holy Spirit into the unity of a most profound harmony of will.

9 Congar, *HDG*, III, 102 points out that from the middle of the twelfth century the theological treatment of the Church was essentially christological and not pneumatological. Consequently, approximately up to the Second Vatican Council, the Church was principally understood as the continuation of the Incarnation, with emphasis on the official institution.

10 Here it may be objected that, after all, Christ, the head, can act without his Bride, the Church: and that consequently the office-bearer can act without the community. In a certain sense, this is in fact a correct but nevertheless an abstract point of view, but on no account a valid basis for a theological description of church office. For, in the first place, there could not be an official action if there were not a Church 'somewhere' in which the office (and the office-bearer) would have its origin and location. Secondly, all official activity, even where a concrete community does not yet exist (for instance in missions or in de-Christianised regions) is related to a community and has significance only in this relationship.

11 This reciprocal interdependence is expressed in many ways, particularly during the celebration of the Eucharist. On the one hand, the priest is a sign that 'the assembly has not the right to control the action which it is performing, that

it is not the lord over the Eucharist: it receives the Eucharist from another, from Christ, who continues to live in his Church': Dombes, I, IX, 35 in *Her-Korr* (1973) 33-29. On the other hand, the office-holder is dependent on the celebrating community. To quote one example from many of the Fathers: Theodore of Mopsuestia, speaking of the salutation 'The Lord be with you' and the response 'and with your spirit', says, 'You (the assembly) answer him (the priest)with an identical prayer. It must then become clear to him and to you all that not only are you in need of the blessing and prayer of the priest, but that he also needs the prayer of all' (quoted by Zizioulas).

12 Similarly, in the theology of the East, St John Chrysostom points out that even an unworthy priest remains an administrator of God's grace: 'He is unworthy? What does that matter? God has made use of bullocks to save his people. It is not the lifestyle of the priest, not his virtue, that accomplishes such things. Everything is a free gift. The priest has only to open his mouth. It is God who accomplishes everything. The priest merely performs the sign. The sacrifice is the same whether it is offered by a chance comer or by Peter or Paul. The one sacrifice is not inferior to the other, since it is not the men who produce its sanctity, but the one who endows it with sanctity'(PG 62:612) cited by J. Danielou. The churches of the Reformation held fast to this view. For example the Augsburg Confession says that even hypocrites and evil men hold office in the Church: 'yet the sacraments are not without effect even when they are being performed by unworthy men: for they represent the person of Christ on account of their calling by the Church: they do not represent their own person, as Christ himself asserted "He who hears you, hears me" (Lk 10:16) When they offer the word of Christ and his sacraments, they are acting in place of Christ. This we learn from that saying of Christ, so that we should not be offended by the unworthiness of the office-bearer'.

13 Cf. H. Urs v. Balthasar, *Amt und Existenz*, 291. And v. Balthasar adds: 'The later heretics, such as the Monantists and Donatists had a correct feeling, although they also drew the wrong conclusion that a Christian priest whose actual life does not reflect the holiness of his office is incapable of transmitting the grace of Christ to the people of God'.

14 The possibility is not excluded that, in individual instances, perseverance in the priestly vocation could become an *intolerable* burden, whether the cause be a failure through personal fault, or a mistaken decision about vocation, or some unforeseeable misfortune (or a combination of all three). Of course, it may be doubted if laicisation, the procedure followed until now, is a suitable solution for such cases. I feel that it is extremely questionable that a very personal decision of conscience should be legitimised, and that a decision be made about a pneumatological sacramental reality by an administrative bureaucratic act. Even though the departure from the priestly ministry has public consequences, it is a most profound personal decision, and in my opinon should be dealt with according to the rules of the internal forum (*Epikie, excusatio a lege*, etc).

15 W. Rohrbach (an Evangelical theologian) writes: 'Celibacy is a sign set up in the freedom which Christ has given to us, a sign of the renunciation of a part of created life, for the sake of a call which makes a radical demand. It is therefore a striking pointer to the eschatological limitation and [merely] relative value of all that is "penultimate", seen in the light of the ultimate reality: and to these"penultimates" belongs the sexual society of husband and wife.' (*Humane Sexualität* (Neukirchen-Vluyn, 1976) 181.

16 The ecclesiastical law of celibacy has had a varied history. Cf. G: Denzler, *Das Papstum und der Amtszölibat*, 2 vols. (Stuttgart 1973 and 1976). The summing up by Schillebeeckx, that the dominant motive for the introduction of a law of continence was 'ritual purity', seems to be questionable. In the evaluation of sources, it is necessary to use clearer principles of critical exegesis in order to distinguish between the *categorisation and verbal expression* of an 'attitude' (which depend on the social and cultural context) and the *'attitude' itself*. Moreover, one must ask what lies 'behind' the idea of 'ritual purity', an idea mostly rejected aprioristically. Could it not be that behind it there is concealed much more of existential experience than a mere depreciation of sexuality?

17 In 'Zwölf Thesen zum Zölibat' in *Christ in der Gegenwart* 33 (1981), G. Lohfink, who is in favour of removing the celibacy law, but on certain definite preconditions, remarks: '(I have) profound sympathy for the expectation of the Church that the preachers of the Gospel should demonstrate radical signs of their following of Christ such as celibacy or renunciation of possessions. For this reason I cannot have an entirely negative attitude to the present celibacy law. In spite of all the incorrect motivations put forward by some — and unfortunately up to the present century the idea of ritual purity has played a disastrous role — it seems to me that in the history of celibacy a more profound, a more certain, instinctive knowledge is expressing something about an inner link between proclamation of the Gospel and the following of Christ'. This link is overlooked by H. Küng in his article 'Ist die Feier ungültig, nur weil der Pfarrer fehlt?', *Deutsches Allgemeines Sonntagsblatt*, 21 June 1981, when he says, 'Wherever a man or a woman possesses sufficient qualification to be a community leader in this particular community, and is also ready to undertake this function, he or she is, according to old Catholic trádition, to be ordained'. Statements of this kind are extremely ambiguous: for 'sufficient qualification' also 'according to old Catholic tradition' includes a real commitment which in a special way shows itself in celibacy.

18 Formerly the life of priestly celibacy had a recognised place in society. Celibacy was not unusual or regarded as offensive, because there were other social ranks and groups whose members normally remained unmarried (teachers, servants, younger sons of farmers etc). Celibacy fitted perfectly into this social context.

19 Moreover, smaller numbers in the new generation of pastors presented the Evangelical Church some years ago with an essentially similar situation which could speak volumes. Although this has changed in the last three or four years, could not this change (coincidentally or not) be related to the great surplus of academic graduates and the ever-increasing difficulty of finding other possible professions?

20 H. Schurmann, *Die Mitte* (Freiburg-Basle-Vienna 1979) 64 writes: 'Somewhere — I no longer know where — I came across the statement that the index of the strength of a person's spiritual life is the way in which he manages his time. In fact, if the law of our life is a loving surrender, what is surrendered first? It is "time". Lovers have time for one another. If we wish well to a person, we must first of all have time for him: we must give him some of our "precious time" which we talk so much about. This is the beginning of all pastoral work. . . . In this context complete self-surrender takes shape, inasmuch as the person no longer holds back any of his time and puts it entirely at the disposal

of God. In such "openness" to God, eternity steps into time, and time becomes transcendent.'

21 O. H. Pesch and A. Peters, *Einführung in die Lehre von Gnade und Rechtfertigung* (Darmstadt 1981) 71. Pesch expressly states 'that in medieval theology there is no pure *habitus entitativus,* which is in no way connected with actual behaviour — no matter what neo-scholasticism may say. Consequently, O. Semmelroth in *Theol Phil* 44 (1969) 185 would prefer to say 'acting in the role of Christ' instead of 'acting *in persona Christi*'. A representation in action is meant.

22 Why make such a distinction if it is unnecessary? Why should not a priest take part in an eucharistic celebration (as a member of the people of God) if another priest is already undertaking the ministry of presiding at the Eucharist? The private Mass is rejected in the Churches of the East: but not alone there. There are instances of the same spiritual tradition is found in the Western Church. For example, St Francis of Assisi writes in his letter to the General Chapter of 1224: 'I exhort and demand in the Lord, that in the house of the Brothers only one Mass in the day is to be celebrated according to the rite of the holy Church. But if there are more priests than one there, for love's sake let the one be satisfied to hear the celebration of the other.' Although also since the Second Vatican Council concelebration on particular occasions is possible and significant, a regularly performed concelebration does not escape the suspicion of 'clericalism', i.e., the attitude that the priest must principally regard himself as distinct from the community, and should not stand also as a lay fellow-Christian, completely in the community. (Quite apart from the fact that some serious theological doubts are to be registered against the present *Western* form of concelebration with the simultaneous recital by all concelebrants of the words of consecration, which thus obscures the sacramental sign of presidency. I should like to examine this question at some time).

23 Originally the priest wore no special form of dress, even when performing liturgical functions. Honoratus, the founder of Lerins, after becoming bishop, prescribed monastic dress for his clergy. Pope Celestine I reproached him for this: 'Those who wear a cloak and a girdle believe that they are observing the faith of Holy Scripture not only in the spirit but also in the letter. . . . We should be distinguished from the people . . . by our teaching, not by our habit, by our conduct not by our clothing, by purity of soul and not by what is external' (PL 50, 431) I owe this reference to R. Zinnhobler, who cites other texts which reject expensive forms of dress for the clergy. J. Gaudemet points out that the *Statuta Ecclesiae antiquae* warn that the cleric should be distinguished from others by his outward simplicity: his spiritual rank should be recognised by the plainness of his dress.

24 Proposed by Prof. Dr W. Breuning, Bonn and Bishop Dr Kl. Hemmerle, Aachen.